THE BOOK OF
COMPARISONS

This Goliath bird-eating spider is shown here at its actual size. Its leg-span is **28cm** – about the size of a large dinner plate.

First published in the UK in 2018 by

Ivy Kids

An imprint of The Quarto Group
The Old Brewery
6 Blundell Street
London N7 9BH
United Kingdom
www.QuartoKnows.com

British Library Cataloguing-in-Publication Data
A catalogue record for this book is available from the British Library.

ISBN: 978-1-78240-558-0

This book was conceived, designed & produced by

Ivy Kids

58 West Street, Brighton BN1 2RA, United Kingdom

PUBLISHER	Susan Kelly
CREATIVE DIRECTOR	Michael Whitehead
MANAGING EDITOR	Susie Behar
ART DIRECTOR	Hanri van Wyk
DESIGNERS	Claire Munday and Kevin Knight
IN-HOUSE DESIGNER	Kate Haynes
PROJECT EDITORS	Leah Willey and Stella Gurney
ASSISTANT EDITOR	Lucy Menzies
FACT CHECKER	Dr Helen Armes, *D.Phil*
EDITORS	Hazel Songhurst and Claire Saunders

CONSULTANTS

Dr Mika Peck *Phd, MSc, BSc 9(hons)*,
Senior Lecturer in Biology, University of Sussex,
Russell Arnott *MOcean PGCE*,
Presenter and Educational Consultant for Incredible Oceans,
Researcher in Phytoplankton Dynamics, University of Bath,
Brian Clegg *MA(Natural Science), MA(Operational Research)*,
Cherith Moses Professor of Geomorphology,
University of Sussex, *FRGS, FGS*.

3 5 7 9 10 8 6 4

THE BOOK OF
COMPARISONS

SIZING UP THE WORLD AROUND YOU

These Little Pygmy Possums from Tasmania are shown here at their actual size, just **5cm** long. Two of them, one on top of the other, would still be shorter than a teaspoon.

CLIVE GIFFORD

ILLUSTRATED BY
PAUL BOSTON

IVY KIDS

CONTENTS

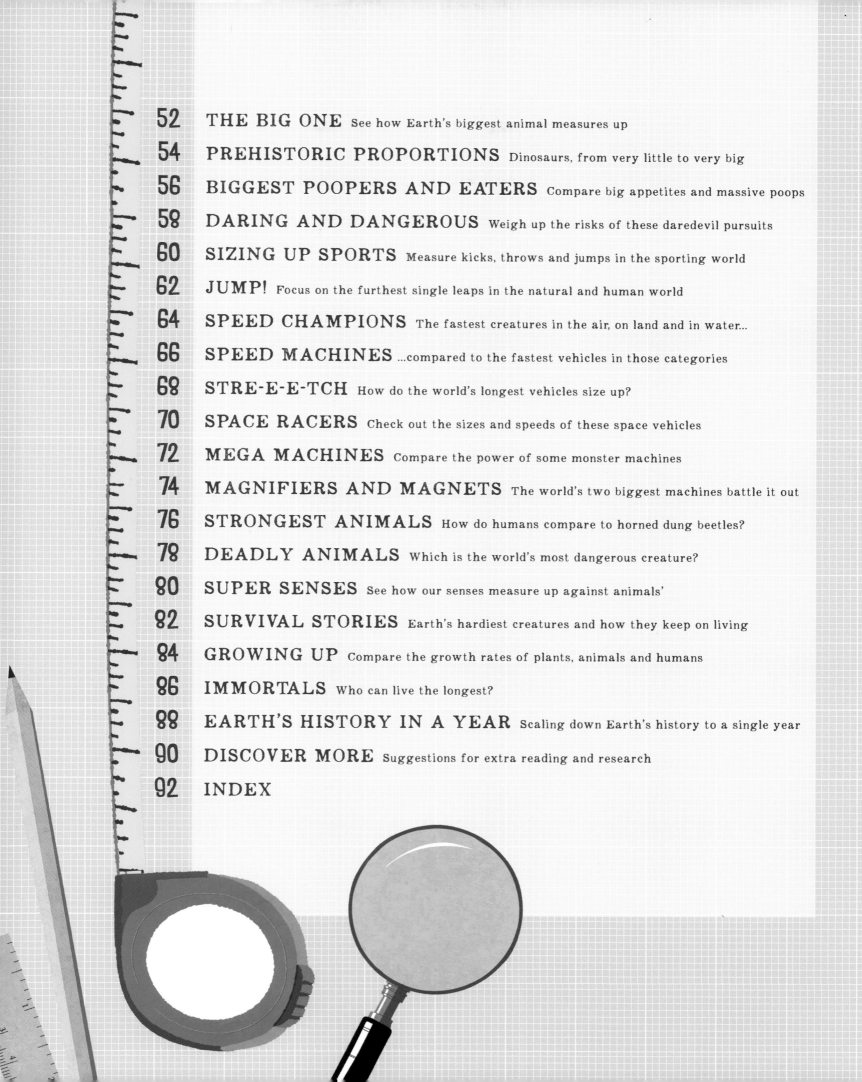

About this book

We compare things around us all the time, from sizing up who's the tallest in your class to picking out the biggest slice of cake in the café. But you don't have to only compare people with people and cake with cake – comparisons can get really wild and weird and wonderful! Take them out with you into the world to see how it measures up. Compare tsunami waves with buildings; trees with jumbo jets and spiders against full stops. Explore the size of mountains against bridges and skyscrapers, or flip them upside down and see how far they'd reach into the deepest places on Earth. Discover how our most powerful machines and creations size up against the forces of nature, or travel way up into the furthest reaches of space to see how our planet looks next to other heavenly bodies. Along the way you'll meet amazing creatures and discover incredible things: the single tree that can store more than 770 bath tubs of water; the species of coral that celebrated its 4,000th birthday over 250 years ago; the adult shark shorter than a pencil…

It's time to look at the world in a whole new way!

The world contains **325 million trillion** gallons of water. That's about the same as 554 trillion Olympic swimming pools.

244.94kph is the record speed of a F1 3-litre powerboat raced by Guido Cappellini in 2005. That's faster than most cars.

A lightning bolt can heat up the air around it to almost **28,000°C**. That's **five** times hotter than the Sun's surface.

At around 7cm long (not including the bill), Anna's hummingbird can fly **385** times its body length each second – faster than a space shuttle re-entering Earth's atmosphere.

Let the comparisons begin...

A typical cumulus cloud can measure 1km across and holds around **500,000 litres** of water.

The biggest-ever recorded tsunami reached the almost unimaginable height of 524 metres. The top speed of tsunamis at sea is over **800kph**... ...that's as fast as some jet aircraft.

The cloud would weigh about as much as **83** elephants.

The highest flying insect is the bumblebee at **9km**, which is higher than the peak of Mount Everest.

A giant squid's eyes are each nearly the size of a football. This helps it to see through the gloom of deeper waters.

The diving peregrine falcon is the world's speediest animal at up to **389kph** – over three times swifter than a cheetah.

The weight of the blue whale's tongue alone is roughly $^2/_3$ the weight of an elephant!

A black marlin was recorded swimming at **129kph**! That's 16kph faster than a cheetah.

How big is BIG?

It's hard to imagine the size of things you have never seen, especially if they're really, really BIG or really, really tiny. Sometimes, a measurement can help… but sometimes it can just look like a meaningless number. So another way to imagine its size is to compare it to things you have seen.

Things that you compare are called 'comparators'. You can choose whatever you want as your comparator – it's fun to use unusual things, such as blue whales and space stations, but you might find it easier to think in pencils or football pitches, or ten-year-olds.

Some comparators have fixed measurements, but most vary. Not all blue whales or ten-year-olds are exactly the same, so we have come up with sizes for these based on lots and lots of research, all approved by our team of experts.

Turn to p.96 to find out more!

People Count

Two thousand years ago, there were around 300 million people on the planet. By 2017, there were 25 times as many – a whopping 7.5 billion!

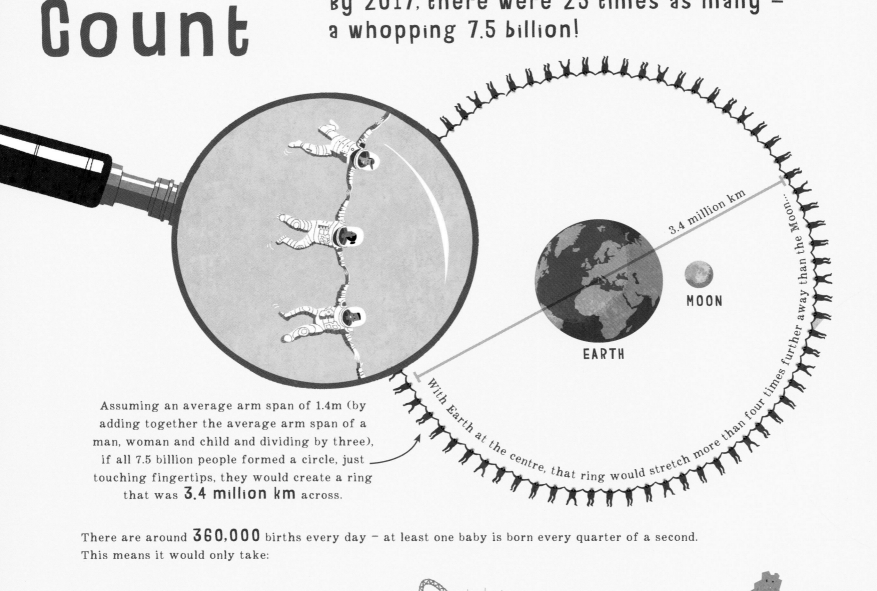

3.4 million km

EARTH

MOON

With Earth at the centre, that ring would stretch more than four times further away than the Moon...

Assuming an average arm span of 1.4m (by adding together the average arm span of a man, woman and child and dividing by three), if all 7.5 billion people formed a circle, just touching fingertips, they would create a ring that was **3.4 million km** across.

There are around **360,000** births every day – at least one baby is born every quarter of a second. This means it would only take:

3 seconds to produce a football team, plus the referee.

6 hours, 7 minutes to fill a huge sports stadium with 88,080 (newborn!) fans.

1 day, 16 hours, 1 minute and 2 seconds to practically equal the population of Luxembourg!

PEOPLE STATS

PEOPLE PYRAMID
The total weight of the human population is about 331 million tonnes, which is 56 times the weight of Egypt's Great Pyramid.

x 56

SMALLEST COUNTRY
The population of Vatican City in Rome, Italy, is just 800 or so. Everyone living there could fit on a single Airbus A380 airliner!

PACKED PLACE
Shanghai, China, is one of the world's most peopled cities. Its population of 24,152,000 is about the same as the whole populaton of Australia.

50.4%
Just over half of the people in the world are male.

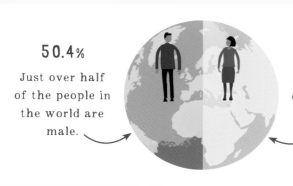

49.6%
Just under half of the people in the world are female.

About a **quarter** of all people are aged 15 or under.

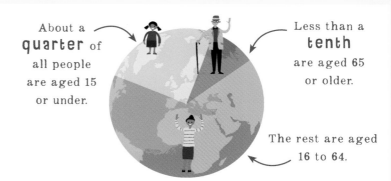

Less than a **tenth** are aged 65 or older.

The rest are aged 16 to 64.

If the world's population was spread out evenly, there would be just **129 people** for approximately every 2.5 square kilometres of land.

2.5 square kilometres

484 American Football fields.

This means that each person in the world...

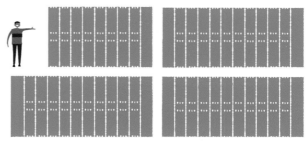

...would have about the same space as **3.7** American Football fields.

In Mongolia there is a lot of land, but not that many people. There are only **five** people for every 2.5 square kilometres.

Macau, in China, is the most crowded place in the world. It crams 55,000 people into each 2.5 square kilometres.

113.6 people would have to fit into just one American Football field!

STILL GROWING
By 2056, the world population is predicted to reach 10 billion.

7.5 billion people	2017
8 billion people	2023
10 billion people	2056

FOOD MOUNTAINS
Every 10 seconds the world population consumes aproximately 856 tonnes of food.

STANDING TALL
If all the people in China stood on each other's shoulders, they would form a tower roughly 2.04 million km tall — that's five times farther than the distance between Earth and the Moon.

Human Dimensions

From a tiny fertilized egg, you develop fast into a bouncing baby girl or boy and you only stop growing in your late teens or early twenties. Let's see how the human body sizes up.

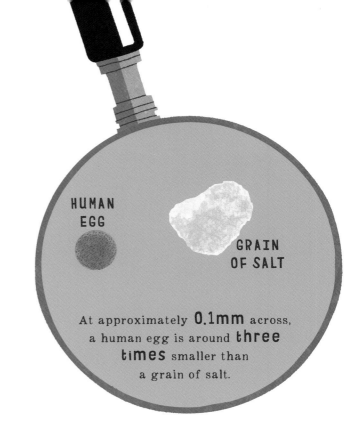

HUMAN EGG

GRAIN OF SALT

At approximately **0.1mm** across, a human egg is around **three times** smaller than a grain of salt.

Some parts of you just keep growing. Fingernails, for instance, grow an average of **3.4mm** per month...

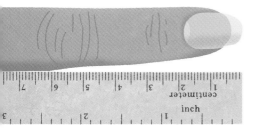

...that's **twice** as quickly as your toenails. It's also the same length as the smallest of the 206 bones in your body — the stapes — which is found in your inner ear.

ACTUAL SIZE STAPES

The femur, or thigh bone, is the biggest bone in the body.

It averages **25–26%** of an adult person's total height.

The femur is **135 times** the length of the stapes...

...and is also around the length of a typical newborn baby.

While people come in all heights, shapes and sizes, some parts of their bodies have similar proportions.

Your forearm

=

about the length of your foot.

Your hand

=

about the length of your face.

Your arm span from fingertip to fingertip

=

roughly the same as your height.

YOUR BRAIN PUTS ON WEIGHT AS YOU GROW FROM A BABY TO AN ADULT.

When you're born, it weighs **350–400g**...

...which is as much as a large grapefruit.

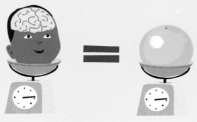

By the time you've grown up, it weighs **1,300–1,400g**...

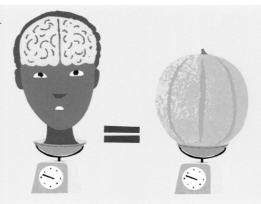

...which is about the same as a large cantaloupe melon.

You have around **650** muscles in your body.

The **smallest** is in your ear, controlling the stapes...

...and the **largest** – the gluteus maximus – is in your bottom!

Digested food is absorbed in your small intestine. This long tube is coiled up inside your body.

If stretched out, it can be as long as **7.3m**...

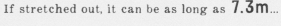

...which is the distance between the goalposts in a full-sized football goal.

The salivary glands in your mouth produce up to **1.5** litres of saliva every day.

In one year, a person could make enough saliva to fill...

...**3.5** bathtubs.

The skin of an adult human weighs **3–4kg**.

If flattened out, it would have an area of roughly **2 metres squared**...

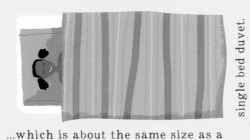

single bed duvet.

...which is about the same size as a

Every day, the blood of an adult human travels **19,000km**.

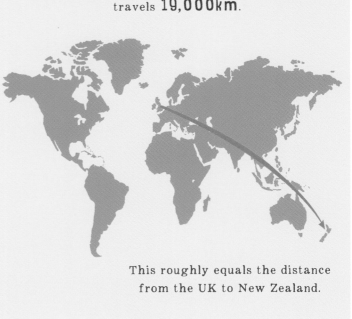

This roughly equals the distance from the UK to New Zealand.

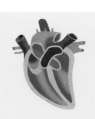

Each heartbeat moves about **70ml** of blood along.

So, at a heart rate of 72 beats per minute, enough blood would be moved in six days...

...to fill the fuel tanks of a Boeing 757.

EARTH'S Energy

The powerful movements of Earth's crust can trigger massive events such as avalanches, tsunamis and earthquakes. All create an awesome amount of energy.

A MIGHTY MOVER

An avalanche can accelerate from a standstill to over **100kph** in just five seconds – as speedily as many sports cars.

A RISING FORCE

Tsunamis are usually caused by underwater disturbances, created by volcanoes or large earthquakes. Tsunami waves in the ocean rarely rise above **2m**, but move with great speed and force. They slow down but increase in size as they travel into shallower coastal waters.

A tsunami in Alaska in 1958 towered over **524m high** – taller than the Empire State Building (without its antenna) with Egypt's Great Pyramid sitting on top!

SERIOUS SNOW SLIDE

In 1970 a massive avalanche on Peru's Mount Huascarán contained **50–100 million cubic metres** of snow, ice and rock...

x 40

...that's enough to fill up Egypt's Great Pyramid 40 times over!

The 2004 Indian Ocean tsunami was caused by a magnitude **9.2** earthquake under the ocean floor. Its energy was estimated to be the equivalent of **4.5 megatons** of TNT explosive...

...that's $1^1/_2$ times the energy of all the explosives and weapons used during World War II.

A wet snow and ice avalanche can travel at **30kph**...

...that's equal to the top speed of a galloping polar bear.

The top speed of a dry snow avalanche is **130kph**...

...that's faster than the maximum speed limit on most highways in the United States.

The top speed of tsunamis at sea is over **800kph**...

...that's as fast as some jet aircraft.

As tsunamis enter shallow water their speed can drop to **32–48kph**...

...about as fast as a racing cyclist.

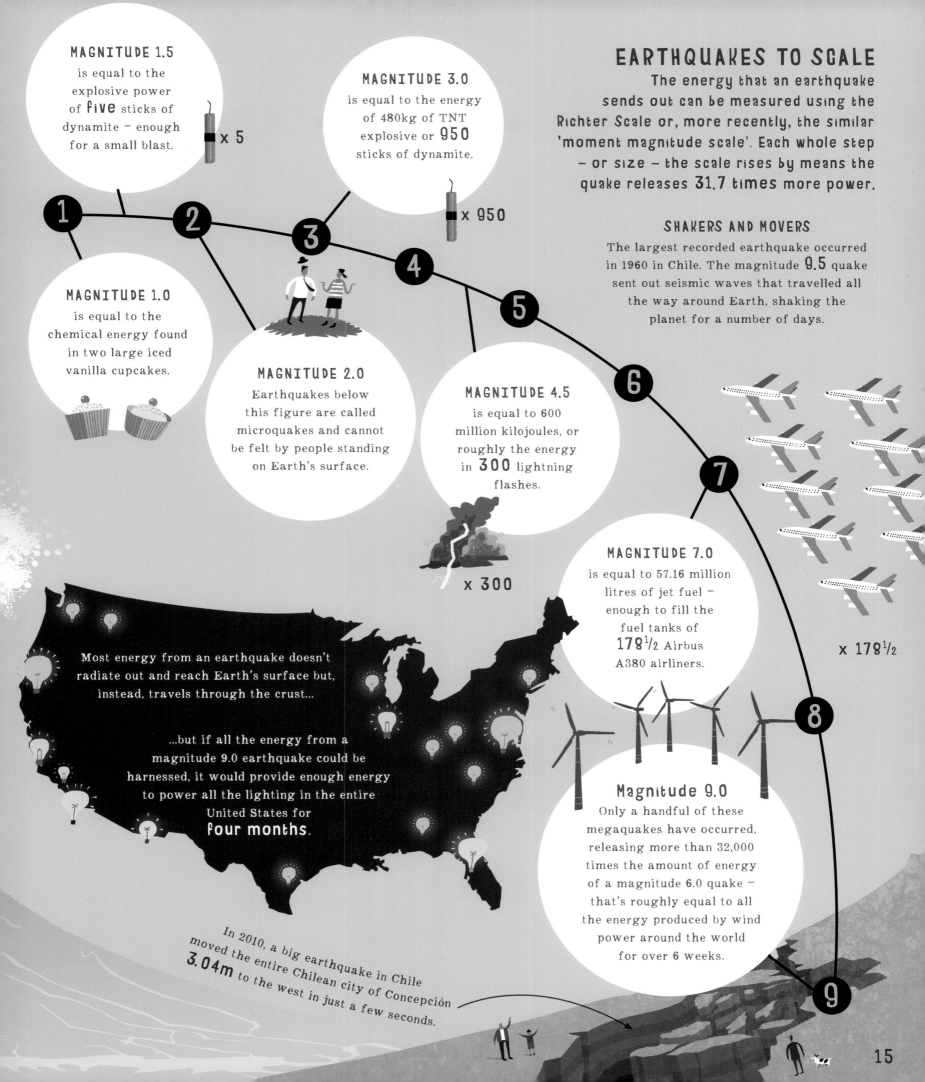

EARTHQUAKES TO SCALE

The energy that an earthquake sends out can be measured using the Richter Scale or, more recently, the similar 'moment magnitude scale'. Each whole step – or size – the scale rises by means the quake releases 31.7 times more power.

MAGNITUDE 1.5
is equal to the explosive power of **five** sticks of dynamite – enough for a small blast.

x 5

MAGNITUDE 3.0
is equal to the energy of 480kg of TNT explosive or **950** sticks of dynamite.

x 950

SHAKERS AND MOVERS
The largest recorded earthquake occurred in 1960 in Chile. The magnitude **9.5** quake sent out seismic waves that travelled all the way around Earth, shaking the planet for a number of days.

MAGNITUDE 1.0
is equal to the chemical energy found in two large iced vanilla cupcakes.

MAGNITUDE 2.0
Earthquakes below this figure are called microquakes and cannot be felt by people standing on Earth's surface.

MAGNITUDE 4.5
is equal to 600 million kilojoules, or roughly the energy in **300** lightning flashes.

x 300

MAGNITUDE 7.0
is equal to 57.16 million litres of jet fuel – enough to fill the fuel tanks of **$178\frac{1}{2}$** Airbus A380 airliners.

x $178\frac{1}{2}$

Most energy from an earthquake doesn't radiate out and reach Earth's surface but, instead, travels through the crust...

...but if all the energy from a magnitude 9.0 earthquake could be harnessed, it would provide enough energy to power all the lighting in the entire United States for **four months**.

Magnitude 9.0
Only a handful of these megaquakes have occurred, releasing more than 32,000 times the amount of energy of a magnitude 6.0 quake – that's roughly equal to all the energy produced by wind power around the world for over 6 weeks.

In 2010, a big earthquake in Chile moved the entire Chilean city of Concepción **3.04m** to the west in just a few seconds.

1 2 3 4 5 6 7 8 9

15

Energetic Examples

Energy is the ability to do work. It can be measured in 'joules'. 1,000 joules equals one kilojoule (kJ). Power is the rate at which energy is used. It is often measured in 'watts'. 1 watt equals 1 joule of energy used for 1 second.

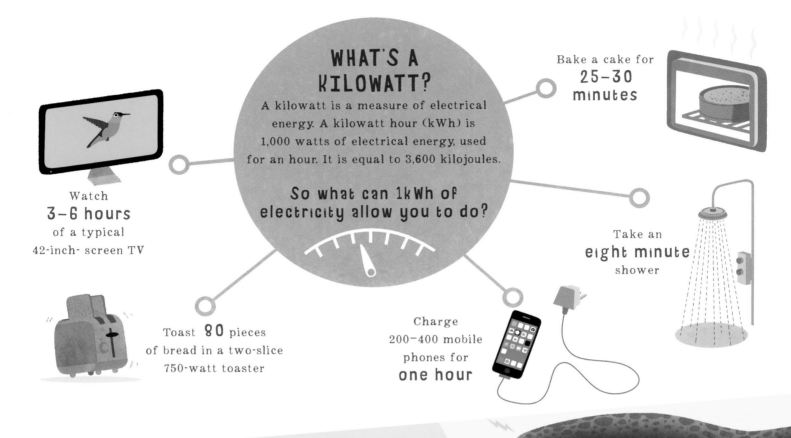

WHAT'S A KILOWATT?

A kilowatt is a measure of electrical energy. A kilowatt hour (kWh) is 1,000 watts of electrical energy, used for an hour. It is equal to 3,600 kilojoules.

So what can 1kWh of electricity allow you to do?

Watch **3–6 hours** of a typical 42-inch- screen TV

Bake a cake for **25–30 minutes**

Take an **eight minute** shower

Toast **80** pieces of bread in a two-slice 750-watt toaster

Charge 200–400 mobile phones for **one hour**

PEDAL POWER

Pedalling a bike for an hour attached to a small electricity generator can produce about **0.1kWh**.

To produce the electricity used in a typical UK house each year (**4,000kWh**), you would need to pedal for **1,666 days** (over 4 and a half years).

LIGHTNING

A bolt of lightning can produce **556kWh** of energy. If it could all be harnessed, it would take **2** lightning strikes to power an average US home for a year.

It would take **135,320** strikes to produce all the electricity Germany uses in one hour.

EEL ENERGY

Electric eels have special cells called electrocytes that, together, can generate around **600 watts** of electricity, but only for a tiny fraction of a second – 2/1000ths to be precise.

If that electricity could be stored and used, you would need:

84 electric eel shocks to power a 100 watt light bulb for just one second.

60,000 shocks to power a 1,200 watt hairdryer for one minute.

2.7 million shocks to power a 900 watt heater for one hour.

ENERGETIC EFFORTS

All creatures, including you, use up energy throughout the day and need to eat food to top it up again.

How much activity would a single banana (weighing 105g and containing 440kJ) fuel for a typical 80kg man?

Walking at 4kph
26 minutes, 25 seconds

Playing table tennis
19 minutes, 48 seconds

Snorkelling
15 minutes, 51 seconds

Disco dancing
10 minutes, 6 seconds

Running at 12kph
6 minutes, 59 seconds

ANIMAL ENERGY
Most creatures use up energy in the act of getting their food.

A hummingbird could expend just **30kJ** a day if it rested all the time (1.25kJ per hour).

A typical banana would keep a resting hummingbird going for 14 days! Hummingbirds, though, spend much of their time flying and use seven times as much energy when hovering in midair.

The three-toed sloth uses the least energy of all mammals. It can use as little as **648kJ** a day. A large slice of pepperoni pizza would contain enough energy (1,380kJ) to keep a three-toed sloth going for two days! (That's if a three-toed sloth ate pizza rather than plant shoots and leaves.)

A cheetah uses around **9,000kJ** of energy a day...

... almost half of it in the 2 hours, 50 minutes on average it spends hunting each day.

A blue whale feeds by lunging forward through the sea and filling its mouth full of water and krill.

Each lunge uses up to **8,071kJ** – equal to almost six large slices of pepperoni pizza.

But the whale can gain an incredible **1,912,088kJ** from a single mouthful of krill. What a meal!

Weather Wonders

Sunny or rainy, mild or wild, the ever-changing weather affects us all. Discover the extremes of this everyday event.

HAILSTONES

These balls of ice form at the tops of very cold clouds and fall to Earth. Most are the size of peas, some the size of golf balls and a few are bigger than grapefruit.

The **largest** hailstone was found in South Dakota, USA in 2010.

Its diameter of over **20cm**...

...made it almost the size of a volleyball.

It weighed **0.88kg**...

...about the weight of **two** soccer balls.

HOT 'N' COLD

14.74°C
was Earth's average temperature over land and sea in 2017.

−89.2°C
was Earth's lowest temperature, measured at Vostok research station in Antarctica in 1983 – that's almost six times colder than Earth's 2017 average temperature.

56.7°C
was Earth's **hottest** temperature, measured at Greenland Ranch, Death Valley, USA, in 1913 – that's around four times hotter than the 2017 average temperature.

HOW WINDY?

Meteorologists sometimes group winds by their speed, using a system called the Beaufort Scale. So how fast do the different winds on the scale move compared to different animals?

Strong breeze
38–49kph...

Gale
62–74kph...

Calm
under 1kph...

Gentle breeze
12–19kph...

...Galapagos giant tortoise

...House mouse

...African elephant

...Ostrich

| 0kph | 13kph | 40kph | 69.9kph |

A typical cumulus cloud can measure **1km** across and holds around **500,000 litres** of water.

The cloud would weigh about as much as **83** elephants.

 **x 83**

STORMY STUFF

The most rain to fall...

...in one minute was **31.2mm** in Maryland, USA, in 1956 — that's enough to submerge your feet in two minutes.

...in one hour was **305mm** in Missouri, USA, in 1947 — that's enough to reach the top of your wellies.

...in 24 hours was over **1,825mm** on Reunion Island, Indian Ocean, in 1966 — that's more rain than your height!

A lightning bolt can heat up the air around it to almost **28,000°C**.

 x5

That's **five** times hotter than the Sun's surface.

SNOW GO!

The biggest single snow crystal to be measured was **10.1mm** wide...

 ...the length of an average housefly.

Snow crystals sometimes clump together to form snowflakes.

 The very largest can be about the size of a dinner plate.

The most snow to fall in 24 hours was **2.56m** in Capracotta, Italy, in 2015...

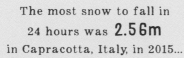

...that's enough to almost bury any creature on land!

A staggering **28.5m** of snow fell in one year at Mount Rainier in the USA...

 ...that's enough to bury the Statue of Liberty (without its base) by about two thirds.

Storm- violent storm
89–117kph...

...Cheetah

Hurricane and tornado
over 118kph...

 ...Racing pigeon

100kph   **120kph**   **140kph**

19

WATER WORLD

Just under one third of the world's surface is dry land. The rest is water – and most of that water is in the oceans.

Earth is known as 'the blue planet' because from space the watery surface looks blue.

The world contains **1,386 million trillion** litres of water. That's about the same as 554 trillion Olympic swimming pools. It is divided up like this:

97%
is the salt water in the seas and oceans.

We can swim and play in salty water, but we can't drink it.

2%
is freshwater that is frozen in the polar ice caps.

We could drink this freshwater, but it's hard to access it.

1%
is freshwater in rivers, lakes, underground, in the air and in living things.

We rely on this much liquid water to stay alive.

IT'S UNIQUE
Water is the only thing on Earth that exists in large amounts in three different states – liquid, solid and gas.

liquid: water

solid: ice

gas: steam or vapour

FEELING THIRSTY?
A human can survive for a month without food, but only for 3–5 days without water.

AFTER YOU
Earth's water is constantly recycled. This means it probably contains traces of the water that dinosaurs drank.

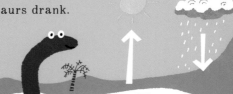

Like all living things, **YOU** are mainly water. Most of it is in the tiny cells that make up every part of your body, from your blood and bones to your organs and skin. The younger you are, the more water your body has in relation to your size.

Your brain is a mind boggling **80%** water. Your cells lose water all the time and can't work properly without regular top ups. That's why it's important to drink water when you exercise – and before a test to boost your brain power!

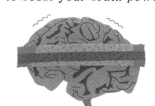

50%

50%   65%   60%   80%

A newborn baby is **75%** water.

The amount of water in an adult man's body is roughly **47.5 x 1 litre** bottles of mineral water.

=

Salt water is heavier than fresh water. The amount of water in a gigantic ocean wave might weigh more than **300 tonnes**.

If a 300-tonne wave fell on you, it would be like **110 SUVs** crash landing on your head all at once.

ASTEROID ATTACK
Most of the world's water developed on Earth. But scientists think water was deposited on Earth around 4 billion years ago by ice-carrying asteroids, during an event called the Late Heavy Bombardment.

TOILET TO TAP?
A quarter of all water used by US households is from flushing toilets. If all the old toilets (22 litres per flush) were replaced with new models (6 litres per flush), then around 2 billion litres of water would be saved every time they were all flushed once.

ALIEN LIFE
Life may have started in hydrothermal vents, openings in the ocean floor that spew superhot water. So will the hot ocean found under ice on Saturn's moon Enceladus be the place to find alien life forms?

Plant Life

Plants range from towering trees large enough to shelter hundreds of people beneath their branches, to plants with features that are too tiny to see without a microscope.

THE GENERAL SHERMAN TREE

Giant sequoias are amongst the biggest, heftiest trees on the planet. One, named the General Sherman Tree, in Northern California, USA, is thought to have first germinated and become a seedling between 2,800 and 2,700 years ago.

The diameter of the largest branch is **2.1m** – about as thick as an adult man balancing a beachball and an orange on his head!

The trunk contains around **1,256 tonnes** of wood. That's the weight of around nine blue whales or almost three fully loaded jumbo jets.

The tree's trunk has a diameter of **11.1m**. A slice of the trunk propped on its side would stand just taller than two giraffes high.

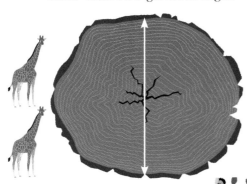

The General Sherman's crown of branches and leaves spreads out an average distance of **32.5m** in all directions...

...that's wider than **two** basketball courts placed side to side.

The General Sherman stands **83.8m** tall – about 1½ times the height of the Leaning Tower of Pisa.

The seed that this giant tree grew from measured just **4–5mm** long and **1mm** wide.

ACTUAL SIZE SEED

The circumference of the trunk measures **31.1m**... ...that's equal to a ring of **21** typical ten-year-old children touching fingertips.

LONGEST LEAF

A species of raffia palm, *Raphia regalis*, boasts big, BIG leaves made up of lots of leaflets. These huge leaves can grow up to **3m** wide and **25.11m** long – about the same length as two giant squid.

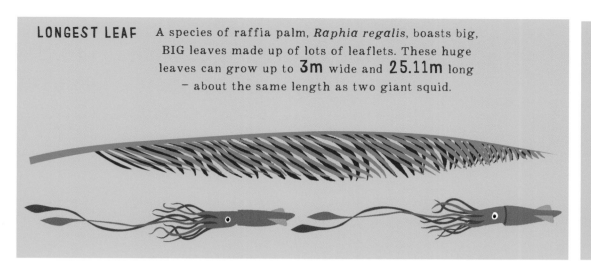

LARGEST LEAF

The *Victoria amazonica* water lily has large round leaves that can grow to a diameter of **2.5m**. The floating leaves can support up to 45kg – more than the weight of a typical 12-year-old child.

SPEEDIEST SEED

about 6cm

about 4cm

The sandbox tree's seeds are stored in pods that violently burst open to disperse the seeds as far as 40m away. The seeds can travel at speeds up to **250kph** – twice as fast as a cheetah!

BIGGEST AND SMALLEST SEEDS

The seed of the coco de mer palm is inside a giant shell that can measure up to **45cm** long and weigh **25kg** – as much as a pair of two-year-old toddlers.

The seeds of some tropical orchids measure just **0.08mm** – smaller than a grain of salt. At only **0.8 micrograms**, it would take 50 or more of these seeds to equal the weight of a human eyelash!

x 50 =

MOST WATER STORAGE

The enormous trunk of the baobab tree measures up to **15.9m** in diameter.

These trees can store vast amounts of water – as much as **120,000 litres** or enough to fill over 774 bath tubs.

x 774

Don't Look DOWN

Do you have a head for heights? Compare the height of a human to the tallest animals on the planet. Then see how the loftiest trees, buildings and mountains on Earth measure up.

HIGH-RISE ANIMALS

Average height of adult male human (1.77m)

MALE GIRAFFE
5.5m

MALE AFRICAN
BUSH ELEPHANT
3.2m

OSTRICH
2.7m

MOOSE
2.1m

POLAR BEAR
1.3m

TOWERING TREES

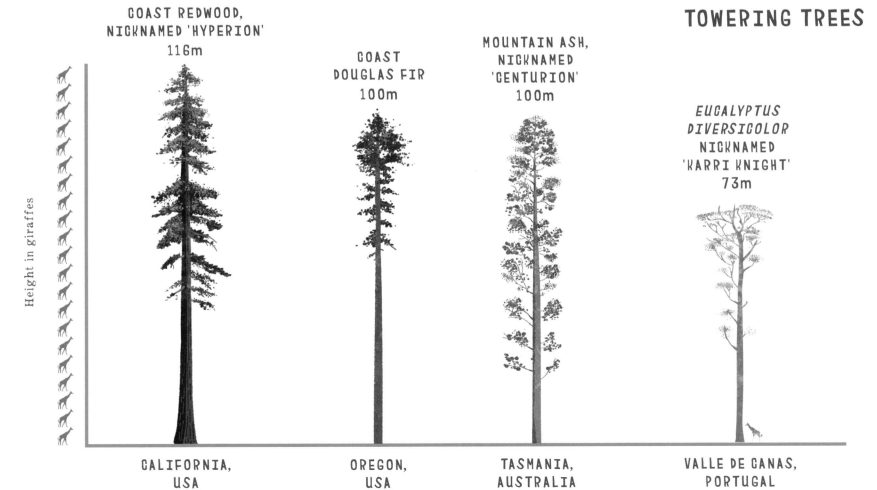

Height in giraffes

COAST REDWOOD,
NICKNAMED 'HYPERION'
116m

COAST
DOUGLAS FIR
100m

MOUNTAIN ASH,
NICKNAMED
'CENTURION'
100m

*EUCALYPTUS
DIVERSICOLOR*
NICKNAMED
'KARRI KNIGHT'
73m

CALIFORNIA,
USA

OREGON,
USA

TASMANIA,
AUSTRALIA

VALLE DE CANAS,
PORTUGAL

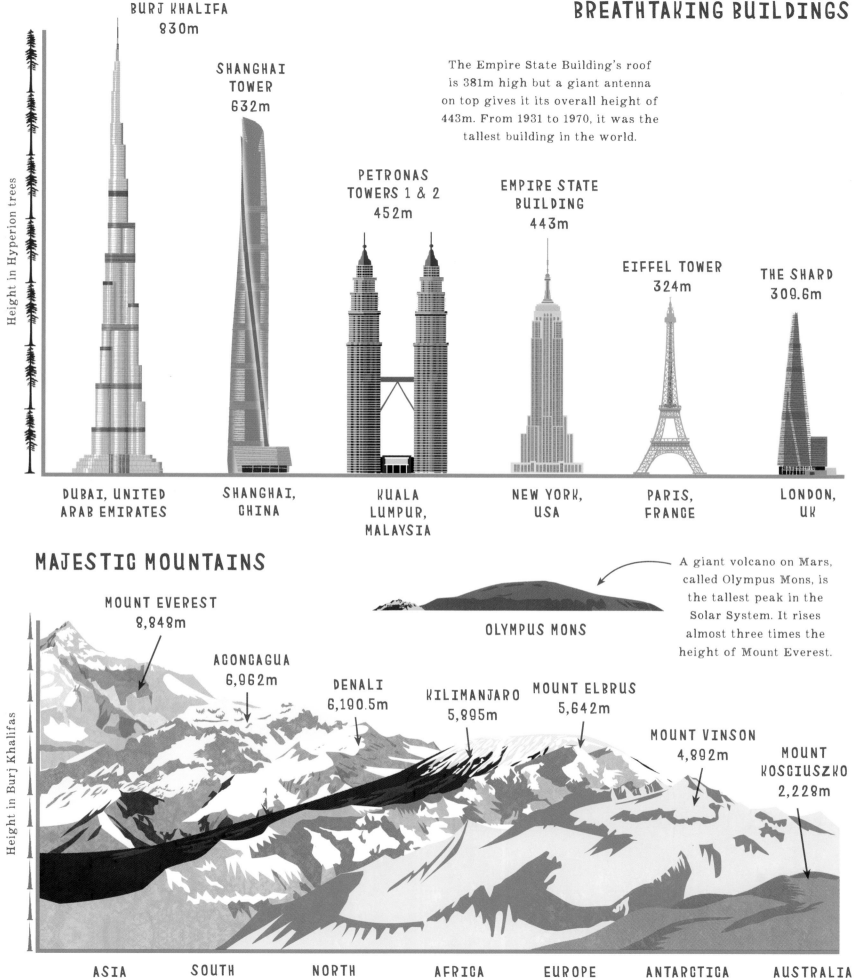

BREATHTAKING BUILDINGS

Height in Hyperion trees

BURJ KHALIFA
830m

SHANGHAI TOWER
632m

The Empire State Building's roof is 381m high but a giant antenna on top gives it its overall height of 443m. From 1931 to 1970, it was the tallest building in the world.

PETRONAS TOWERS 1 & 2
452m

EMPIRE STATE BUILDING
443m

EIFFEL TOWER
324m

THE SHARD
309.6m

DUBAI, UNITED ARAB EMIRATES

SHANGHAI, CHINA

KUALA LUMPUR, MALAYSIA

NEW YORK, USA

PARIS, FRANCE

LONDON, UK

MAJESTIC MOUNTAINS

Height in Burj Khalifas

MOUNT EVEREST
8,848m

ACONCAGUA
6,962m

DENALI
6,190.5m

KILIMANJARO
5,895m

MOUNT ELBRUS
5,642m

MOUNT VINSON
4,892m

MOUNT KOSCIUSZKO
2,228m

OLYMPUS MONS

A giant volcano on Mars, called Olympus Mons, is the tallest peak in the Solar System. It rises almost three times the height of Mount Everest.

ASIA

SOUTH AMERICA

NORTH AMERICA

AFRICA

EUROPE

ANTARCTICA

AUSTRALIA

Awesome Altitudes

Say "hi" to these amazing heights. Choose a scale – kilometres or pencils!

Altitude scale labels (pencils)

- 2,106,163,157 pencils.
- 2,023,157,895 pencils.
- 613,589,473 pencils.
- 2,289,473 pencils.
- 198,158 pencils.
- 184,437 pencils.
- 110,668 pencils.

Features

APOLLO 13 ASTRONAUTS
Highest humans
400,171km

MOON
384,400km

VELA 2 SATELLITE
Highest Earth satellite
116,582km

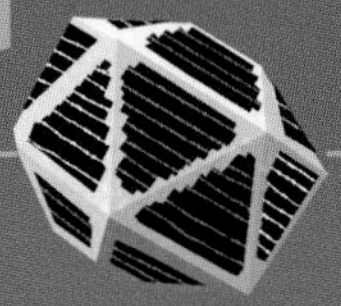

ISS
The International Space Station orbits Earth at an altitude of **330–435km.**

HIGHEST PLANE FLIGHT
MIG 25 jet aircraft
37.6km

HIGHEST BALLOON
21km
This 2005 trip over India was in a 48m high balloon – two metres taller than the Statue of Liberty minus its base.

HIGHEST PAPER PLANE
Stratos III
35km
The plane was released from a floating helium balloon and glided back to Earth.

An average pencil contains enough graphite to draw a line up to 56km long – more than **six times** the height of Mount Everest!

Altitude scale (km)

- 400,000km
- 300,000km
- 200,000km
- 100,000km
- 600km
- 400km
- 200km
- 50km
- 40km
- 30km
- 20km

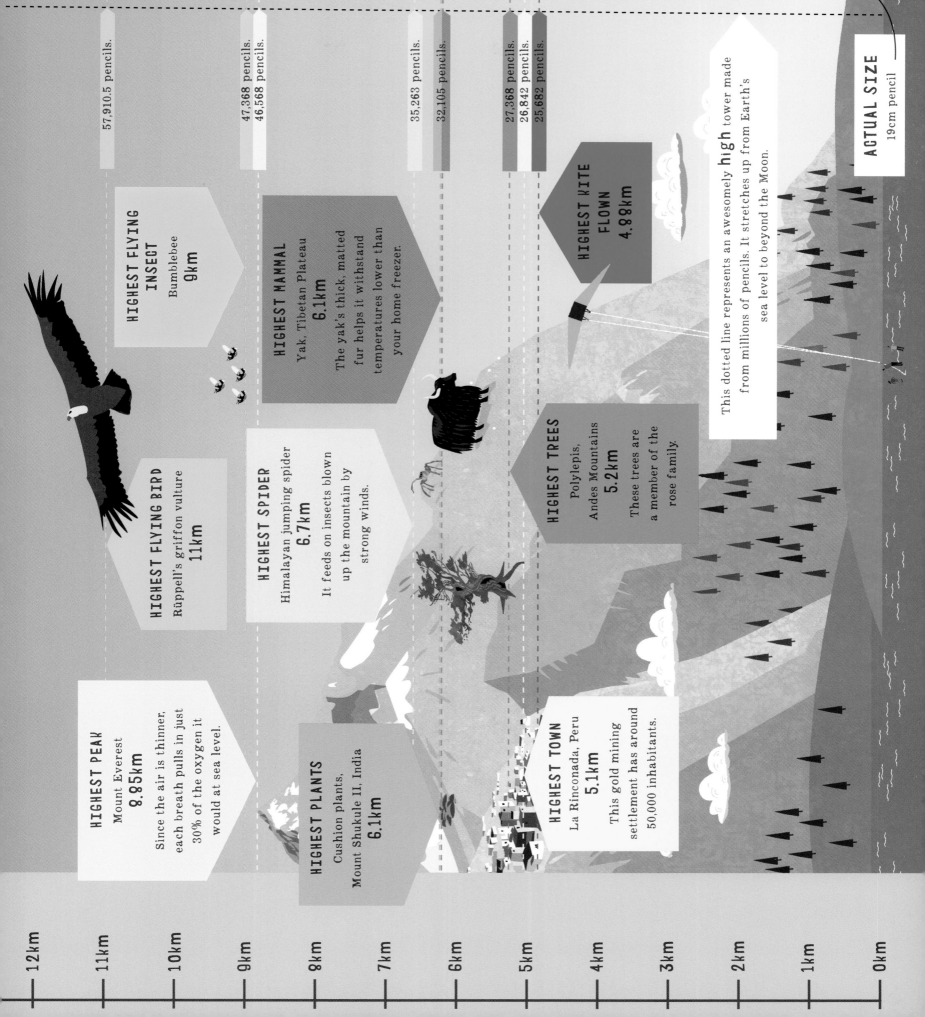

HIGHEST PEAK
Mount Everest
8.85km

Since the air is thinner,
each breath pulls in just
30% of the oxygen it
would at sea level.

HIGHEST PLANTS
Cushion plants,
Mount Shukule II, India
6.1km

HIGHEST TOWN
La Rinconada, Peru
5.1km

This gold mining
settlement has around
50,000 inhabitants.

HIGHEST FLYING
INSECT
Bumblebee
9km

HIGHEST MAMMAL
Yak, Tibetan Plateau
6.1km

The yak's thick, matted
fur helps it withstand
temperatures lower than
your home freezer.

HIGHEST KITE
FLOWN
4.88km

HIGHEST FLYING BIRD
Rüppell's griffon vulture
11km

HIGHEST SPIDER
Himalayan jumping spider
6.7km

It feeds on insects blown
up the mountain by
strong winds.

HIGHEST TREES
Polylepis,
Andes Mountains
5.2km

These trees are
a member of the
rose family.

57,910.5 pencils.

47,368 pencils.
46,568 pencils.

35,263 pencils.
32,105 pencils.

27,368 pencils.
26,842 pencils.
25,682 pencils.

This dotted line represents an awesomely **high** tower made
from millions of pencils. It stretches up from Earth's
sea level to beyond the Moon.

ACTUAL SIZE
19cm pencil

12km
11km
10km
9km
8km
7km
6km
5km
4km
3km
2km
1km
0km

Hidden Depths

Earth's surface may be a busy and exciting place, but there are also some surprising discoveries to be made DEEP underground.

DEPTH IN METRES

0
100
200
300
400
500
600
700
800
900
1,000
1,100
1,200
1,300
1,400
1,500
1,600

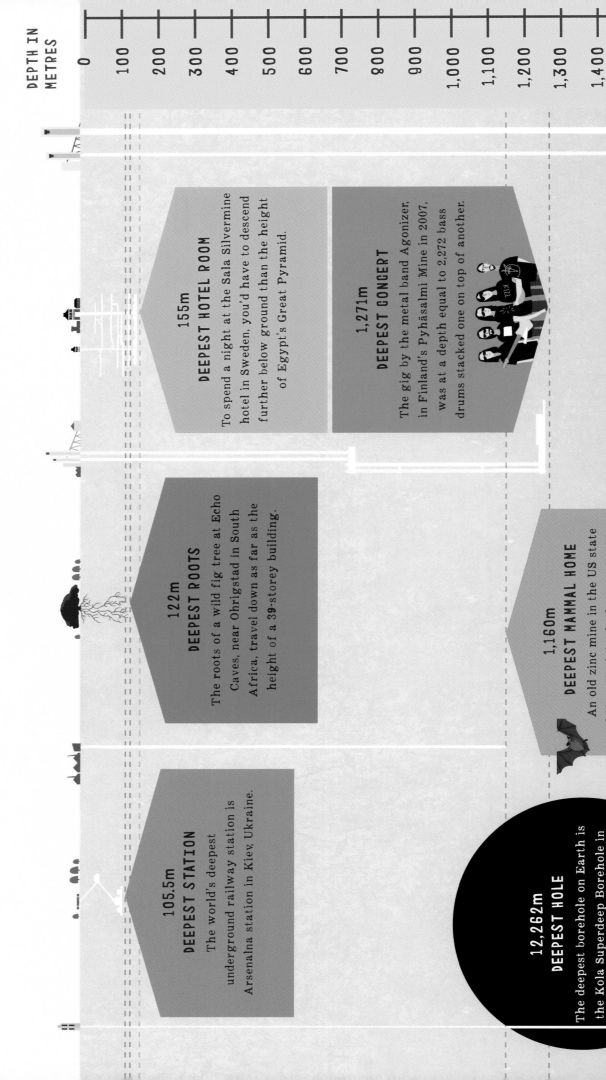

155m
DEEPEST HOTEL ROOM

To spend a night at the Sala Silvermine hotel in Sweden, you'd have to descend further below ground than the height of Egypt's Great Pyramid.

1,271m
DEEPEST CONCERT

The gig by the metal band Agonizer, in Finland's Pyhäsalmi Mine in 2007, was at a depth equal to 2,272 bass drums stacked one on top of another.

122m
DEEPEST ROOTS

The roots of a wild fig tree at Echo Caves, near Ohrigstad in South Africa, travel down as far as the height of a 39-storey building.

1,160m
DEEPEST MAMMAL HOME

An old zinc mine in the US state of New York is the home to 1,000 little brown bats each winter. They live at a depth equal to 1.4 times the height of the world's tallest building, the Burj Khalifa.

105.5m
DEEPEST STATION

The world's deepest underground railway station is Arsenalna station in Kiev, Ukraine.

12,262m
DEEPEST HOLE

The deepest borehole on Earth is the Kola Superdeep Borehole in Russia. It is equal to the height of 1.4 Mount Everests.

1,900 2,000 2,100 2,200 2,300 2,400 2,500 2,600 2,700 2,800 2,900 3,000 3,100 3,200 3,300 3400 3,500 3,600 3,700 3,800 3,900 4,000

2,283m
LONGEST LIFT JOURNEY

The Mponeng gold mine in South Africa features the world's deepest lift. It can carry 120 people and travel at speeds of up to 64kph.

2,800m
DEEPEST LIVING BACTERIA

Deep in the Mponeng gold mine, is a species of bacteria called *Desulforudis*. At just 0.004mm long, you would need 25 of them, laid end-to-end, to equal the thickness of this page.

4,000m
DEEPEST MINE

Eight of the world's ten deepest mines are gold mines located in South Africa. TauTona is the very deepest – stretching 10.5 times the height of the Empire State Building (minus antenna) below ground.

2,197m
DEEPEST CAVE

Krubera Cave in the former Soviet state of Georgia, is the deepest cave on Earth. Springtail insects were found living in it at 1,980m. Travelling that distance on a typical escalator would take 66 minutes!

3,600m
DEEPEST CREATURE

The deepest-dwelling creature ever discovered was a species of roundworm found in South African gold mines. The roundworm are just 0.5–0.56mm long – just under the size of two single grains of table salt.

2,256m
DEEPEST DINOSAUR

Found in Norway, a knucklebone of a plateosaur is the deepest dinosaur fossil found anywhere in the world, buried at a depth equal to seven Eiffel Towers stacked on top of each other.

HOT ROCKS

In the depths of the mine, the temperature is much higher as it's nearer Earth's hot core. Some of the rocks can reach over 60°C – double that above ground and just about enough to fry an egg on the rock! More than 5,400 tonnes of ice – the same weight as 42 blue whales – are used each day to help cool down the deepest parts of the mine.

Undersea Life

The world's seas and oceans teem with hundreds of thousands of plant and marine species living at different depths of the ocean – we probably only know less than a third of them!

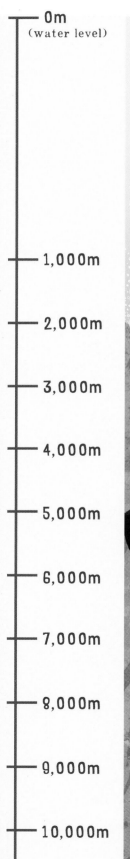

2–50m
The porcupine pufferfish is poisonous and covered in vicious prickles. It sucks in sea water to treble in size.

300–600m
A giant squid's eyes are each about the size of a football. This helps it to see through the gloom of deeper waters.

0–60m
Tropical coral reefs flourish in shallow waters. They are home to as much as 25% of all known fish.

1,500–5,800m
Hydrothermal vents are gaps in the ocean crust where the water is heated up to 400°C and full of minerals. Some minerals form chimneys around the vent. One grew as tall as a 15-storey building.

3,000–4,000m
Dumbo octopuses have large fins that look like elephant ears. They hover above ocean floors, sucking up worms and other small creatures.

3,700m
Most jellyfish are found near the surface, but in 2016, scientists discovered a new type of deep-sea jellyfish that looks like a flying saucer with tentacles.

5,762m
The deepest shipwreck ever found was of the SS *Rio Grande*, which sank in the Atlantic during World War II.

6,000–9,000m
Shrimp-like amphipods are normally 1–2cm long. But deep-ocean amphipods can be super giant – up to 20 times as big.

8,372m
The deepest fish ever found was a type of cusk eel called *Abyssobrotula galatheae*.

DIVERS
Some animals can dive to seriously impressive depths.

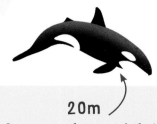

100m
Lionfish can eat up to 20 fish in 30 minutes, which can make their stomach 30 times bigger!

332.35m
Egyptian diving instructor, Ahmed Gabr, plunged to this world record depth in 2014.

20m
Orcas spend most of their time in the top 20m of the ocean but can dive down swiftly to 100m.

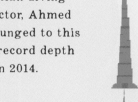

300–1,000m
Lanternfish create their own light source via chemical reactions in their body. At night, they swim up to feed in the top 100m of the ocean, using their lights to attract prey.

400–2,000m
Sperm whales are the ocean's largest carnivores. They eat fish, seals and squid, sometimes diving to a depth of 2,000m to chase prey.

2,338m
The southern elephant seal dives to a depth of five times the height of the Empire State Building.

2,992m
Cuvier's beaked whale is the deepest diving mammal. One was spotted at 2,992m beneath the Pacific Ocean, in a dive lasting $137\frac{1}{2}$ minutes.

If **Mount Everest** was placed on Challenger Deep, its peak would still be over 2.1km under water.

In fact, you could place two of the world's tallest building (the Burj Khalifa) on top of Mount Everest plus the Empire State Building and there would *still* be water above!

Only three people have ever descended below 10,000m, the latest being James Cameron in his Deepsea Challenger craft in 2012. He reached 10,908m below sea level in Challenger Deep.

10,994m
Challenger Deep, in the Pacific, is the deepest point of the world's oceans.

Hot 'n' cold

Temperatures vary wildly around the planet – from scorching to freezing. Explore and compare the hottest and coldest air temperatures on each continent as well as adaptions by people and creatures to living life in extreme temperatures.

Most creatures die if their body freezes but not the Alaskan wood frog (*Rana sylvatica*). In winter temperatures even colder than −10°C, the frog's blood can freeze and its heart stop for months yet it will revive itself in spring!

The temperature of lava during an eruption of the Kīlauea volcano in Hawaii is about 1,170°C – over 20½ times the hottest weather temperature recorded at Death Valley in California.

• Snag, Yukon, Canada

North America coldest: −63°C

NORTH AMERICA

North America hottest: 56.7°C

• Death Valley, California

ATLANTIC OCEAN

EQUATOR

SOUTH AMERICA

South America hottest: 48.9°C

• Rivadavia, Argentina

PACIFIC OCEAN

South America coldest: −32.8°C

Sarmiento, Argentina •

Antarctica hottest: 17.5°C

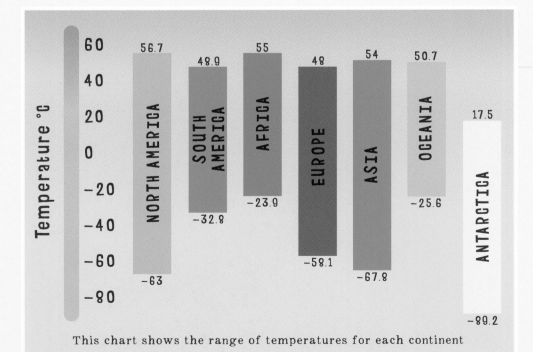

This chart shows the range of temperatures for each continent

	North America	South America	Africa	Europe	Asia	Oceania	Antarctica
Hottest	56.7	48.9	55	48	54	50.7	17.5
Coldest	−63	−32.8	−23.9	−58.1	−67.8	−25.6	−89.2

Icefish have see-through blood containing substances which act as anti-freeze. This enables the fish to survive temperatures below freezing. One in nine of all fish around the continental shelf of Antarctica are icefish.

Esperanza Research Station

In 2012, an experiment at CERN's Large Hadron Collider generated a temperature of over **5 trillion °C** – the hottest-ever temperature on Earth. That incredible temperature is 333,333 times hotter than the centre of the Sun!

Russia is such a huge country that it spans Europe and Asia. In some years, temperatures in this isolated Russian town drop below 0°C in September and stay below freezing until May. Children here have to be especially hardy as school only closes if the temperature reaches **−52°C**.

Asia
coldest:
−67.8°C

Europe
coldest:
−58.1°C

PACIFIC
OCEAN

Oymyakon, Russia

• Ust'Shchuger,
Russia

Europe
hottest:
48.0°C

EUROPE

Asia
hottest:
54.0°C

ASIA

To escape the temperatures in summer of **35−45°C**, most of the residents of the opal mining town of Coober Pedy in South Australia live underground in homes burrowed out of the rock. There, the temperature remains a more manageable 24°C or so. The town even contains underground hotels and churches.

Ifrane,
Morocco •   Athens, Greece •

Kebili,
Tunisia •

• Tirat Tsvi, Israel

Africa
coldest:
−23.9°C

Africa
hottest:
55.0°C

AFRICA

In 2005, the desert ground of Dasht-e Lut in Iran absorbed so much heat from the Sun that the land surface temperature was measured **70.7°C** – the hottest place on Earth.

OCEANIA

Oceania
hottest:
50.7°C

INDIAN
OCEAN

Oodnadatta,
Australia

Coober Pedy,
Australia

The African bullfrog buries itself underground to escape the heat in a sac made of mucus, which hardens in the hot, dry weather. It can stay there for as long as seven years without water, waiting for the rains to come. The frog can weigh as much as 2kg – the weight of two hedgehogs.

Ranfurly,
New Zealand •

SOUTHERN
OCEAN

Antarctica
coldest:
−89.2°C

Oceania
coldest:
−25.6°C

ANTARCTICA

Vostok Research Station •

Earth's LONGEST

Some things can stretch to quite extraordinary lengths. Let's look at some long, looooong landmarks, both natural and human-made.

The Andes

in South America is the longest mountain range on Earth. It stretches for roughly...

...7,000km.

7,000km is about the same distance between Rome, in Italy, and New York, USA.

THE NILE RIVER

flows from south to north through parts of Africa, for a distance of...

...6,695km.

That's almost **16** times the length of the Grand Canyon in the USA, or the length of almost **159** marathon runs.

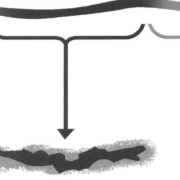

676km
LAKE TANGANYIKA

in eastern Africa is the longest freshwater lake in the world.

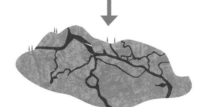

651.78km
THE MAMMOTH CAVE

in Kentucky, USA, is the world's longest cave system. Since it hasn't all been mapped, it may be even longer!

504.6km
YARLUNG TSANGPO GRAND CANYON

is in Tibet. It is 61km longer than the Grand Canyon in the USA.

979m
KEREPAKUPAI MERÚ

or Angel Falls, in Venezuela, is the world's highest waterfall, and just over three times the height of the Eiffel Tower.

400km
THE LAMBERT-FISHER GLACIER

in Antarctica is more than twice the length of the 190km Bering Glacier in Alaska — the longest in the USA.

254km
THE PRAIA DO CASSINO

beach in Brazil is double the length of Cox's Bazar beach in Bangladesh.

The Andes would fit **two thirds** of the way around the Moon.

The Andes would cover a distance **greater** than half the diameter of Earth.

The Andes would stretch **farther** than the diameter of Mars.

Moon's circumference
══ 10,917km

Earth's diameter
══ 12,756km

Mars' diameter
══ 6,792km

LONG STRUCTURES

Some super-long structures have been built around the world, mostly to carry water, goods or people around. Here are the loooongest...

164.8km

The Danyang–Kunshan Grand Bridge, China, carries high-speed trains between the Chinese cities of Shanghai and Nanjing.

170km

The Delaware Aqueduct, USA, carries water to New York City. It is more than two and a half times the length of the world's longest transport tunnel in Guangzhou, China, which carries metro trains.

1,776km

The Grand Canal, China, joins the Yellow and Yangtze rivers. Building began on it over 1,500 years ago.

9,289km

The Trans–Siberian Railway, Russia, runs from Moscow to Vladivostok. It has more than 440 bridges and 39 tunnels.

48,000km

The Pan–American Highway runs through 14 countries, from Prudhoe Bay, Alaska, to the southernmost tip of Argentina.

EXTREME Journeys

Journeys don't have to be short, routine or boring. Here are some extreme examples of tough trips, epic treks and massive migrations made by people and creatures around the planet and beyond!

MEGA MIGRATIONS

Some creatures go to incredible lengths to breed, find fresh places to eat or seek out winter warmth. Here are ten of these amazing migrations.

 Ruby-throated hummingbird – **2,200km**

Salmon – up to **3,800km**

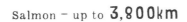 Monarch butterfly – **4,000km**

Grant's caribou – **4,800km**

Humpback whale – **8,300km**

Adélie penguin – **13,000km**

Painted lady butterfly – **15,000km**

 Globe skimmer dragonfly – **18,000km**

Leatherback turtle – **20,500km**

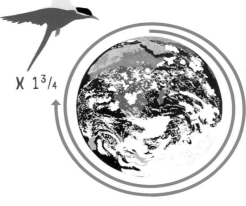
X 1³/₄

Arctic tern
71,000km —
that's once and three-quarters around Earth!

However, no single painted lady completes the whole migration cycle. New butterflies develop and old butterflies die on the way. It can take six generations to make the entire **15,000km** trip.

WANDERERS AND MOVERS

FREE FLIER
The wandering albatross is well named. This giant bird can soar above the ocean on single 15,000-km flights – that's like travelling from Houston in Texas, USA, to Perth in Australia.

CRAB-TASTIC
Every October to December, Christmas Island turns red as 40–50 million red crabs swarm from its forests to breed on the coast. Specially-built bridges and tunnels allow the crabs to reach the beaches safely.

ONE-WHEEL WONDER

In 2002, Lars Clausen rode a unicycle 14,686.82km to make a double-crossing of the US, from the West Coast to the East Coast and back again. He made 5,118,000 pedal turns during his 205-day journey.

LONGEST JOURNEYS
Humans also make some pretty epic journeys, by land, sea and air.

4,800km The longest journey made by a wind-powered car, the *Wind Explorer*, was across Australia from Albany to Sydney.

10,267km The train trip from Moscow, Russia, to Pyongyang, North Korea, takes up to 207 hours.

12,501km The *RTE Nord* log raft made this non-stop voyage across the Pacific in 2002–03, taking 136 days.

14,534km As of 2017, the longest scheduled non-stop flight is Auckland, New Zealand, to Doha, Qatar, taking 18 hours and 20 minutes.

30,608km The longest, unbroken walk was from Tierra del Fuego, at the southern tip of Argentina, to Prudhoe Bay, Alaska.

57,085km The longest non-stop undersea submarine voyage was made in 1982–83 by HMS *Warspite*. The military submarine stayed submerged and on patrol for 111 days in the South Atlantic.

Valeri Polyakov made the longest-ever journey by a living thing in 1994–95, when he spent **437 days, 18 hours** on board the Russian Mir space station, orbiting Earth. During his journey on board Mir, Polyakov orbited Earth 7,075 times. He travelled 300,765,472km – that's further than travelling from Earth to the Sun and back.

A MASS MIGRATION
Every year in Africa, thousands of animals travel across the plains of the Serengeti and Masai Mara in Kenya and Tanzania. They make this circular journey, up to **1,600km** in distance, to reach fresh grazing lands.

More than 200,000 zebras and 300,000 Thomson's gazelle make the trip, along with around 1.4 million wildebeest.

If all the zebras on the migration stood on each other's backs, they would form a tower **260,000m** high – more than 29 times higher than Mount Everest.

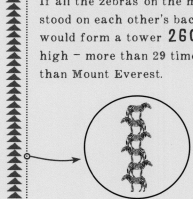

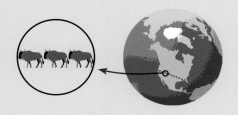

If all the wildebeest stood nose to tail, the queue would stretch **3,360km** – enough to cross the USA coast-to-coast from San Diego, California, to Jacksonville Beach, Florida.

LONG WAY HOME
In 1923, the Brazier family's pet dog, Bobbie, got lost on a family trip to Wolcott, Indiana. The family returned home to Silverton, Oregon and six months later, so did Bobbie! He had somehow made the epic journey of around 4,250km across the United States.

EPIC SWIM
In 2007, Slovenia's Martin Strel swam 5,265km down the Amazon River, alongside crocodiles, anacondas and piranhas, in a lung-busting 66 days. His swimming distance was almost 150km further than travelling from New York City in America to Dublin in Ireland.

Our Place in Space

Earth is the third planet from the Sun, and one of the eight planets of the Solar System – our little bit of the Universe.

Jupiter is the biggest planet in the Solar System. If it was the size of a 25cm-diameter watermelon, then Earth would be a 2cm-wide cherry tomato and the Moon about the size of a single kernel of sweetcorn. More than 1,300 planet Earths could fit inside Jupiter.

JUPITER
142,984km diameter
Watermelon

SATURN
120,536km diameter
Large grapefruit

NEPTUNE
49,528km diameter
Apple

Pluto is now called a dwarf planet and, at 2,370km in diameter, would be the size of a peppercorn.

MERCURY
4,879km
Blueberry

URANUS
51,118km
Medium orange

VENUS
12,104km
Cherry tomato

EARTH
12,756km
Cherry tomato

MARS
6,792km
Blueberry

AVERAGE SURFACE TEMPERATURES OF THE PLANETS

VENUS	MERCURY	EARTH	MARS	JUPITER	SATURN	URANUS	NEPTUNE
464°C	167°C	15°C	−65°C	−110°C	−140°C	−195°C	−200°C

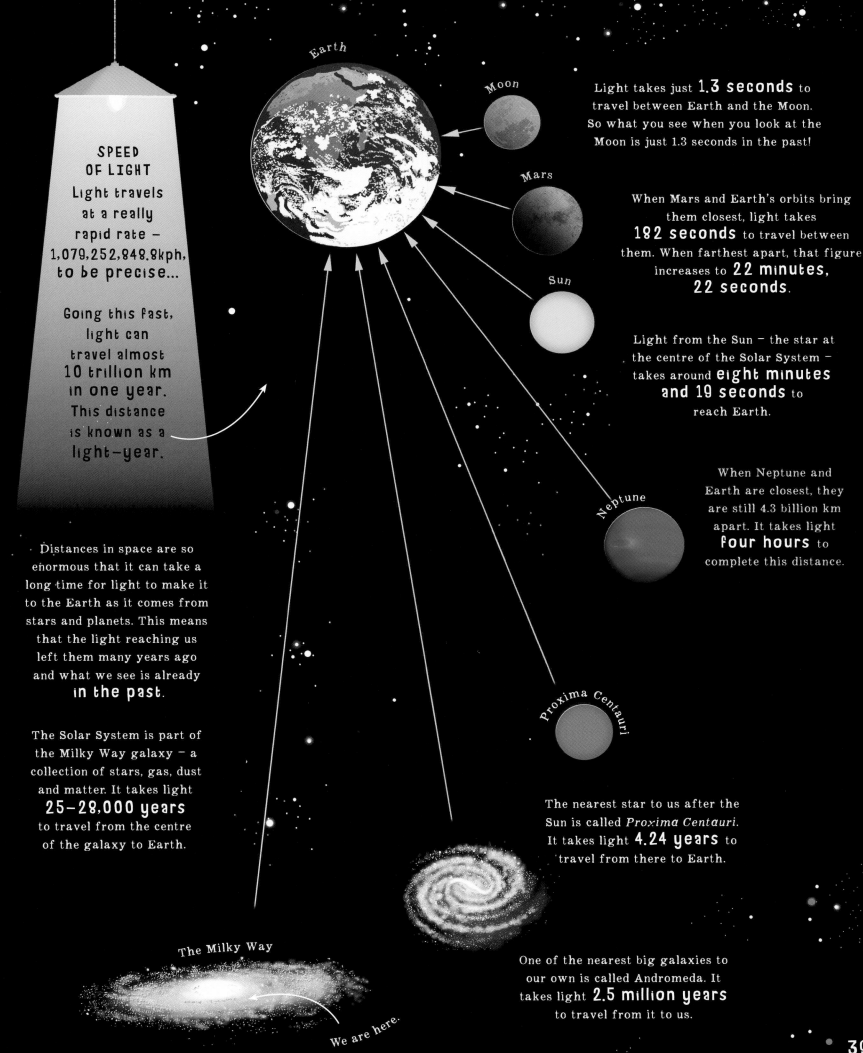

SPEED OF LIGHT
Light travels at a really rapid rate – 1,079,252,848.8kph, to be precise...

Going this fast, light can travel almost 10 trillion km in one year. This distance is known as a light-year.

Distances in space are so enormous that it can take a long time for light to make it to the Earth as it comes from stars and planets. This means that the light reaching us left them many years ago and what we see is already **in the past**.

The Solar System is part of the Milky Way galaxy – a collection of stars, gas, dust and matter. It takes light **25–28,000 years** to travel from the centre of the galaxy to Earth.

Earth

Moon

Light takes just **1.3 seconds** to travel between Earth and the Moon. So what you see when you look at the Moon is just 1.3 seconds in the past!

Mars

When Mars and Earth's orbits bring them closest, light takes **182 seconds** to travel between them. When farthest apart, that figure increases to **22 minutes, 22 seconds**.

Sun

Light from the Sun – the star at the centre of the Solar System – takes around **eight minutes and 19 seconds** to reach Earth.

Neptune

When Neptune and Earth are closest, they are still 4.3 billion km apart. It takes light **four hours** to complete this distance.

Proxima Centauri

The nearest star to us after the Sun is called *Proxima Centauri*. It takes light **4.24 years** to travel from there to Earth.

The Milky Way

We are here.

One of the nearest big galaxies to our own is called Andromeda. It takes light **2.5 million years** to travel from it to us.

Space is a BIG Place

You may think Earth is a pretty big place but it's incredibly tiny and titchy compared to the rest of the Universe. Let's go seriously up in scale as we explore the enormity of space.

The Solar System journeys through space at a rapid 230km every second...

...if you were to travel at that speed, it would take you just 2 minutes and 54 seconds to get all the way around Earth and back again!

Even at that, speed it takes the Solar System 230 million years to complete an orbit around the Milky Way.

LOC

DIAMETE

MILKY WAY
DIAMETER: 100,000 light-years

SOLAR SYSTEM
DIAMETER: 29.9 billion km
(0.0032 light-years)

EARTH
DIAMETER: 12.756km

You would need to line up
2,343,995
planet Earths in a row to equal the diameter of the Solar System.

There is not a clear definition of where the Solar System ends, but NASA uses the extent of the 'solar wind', which is the flow of particles from the Sun. These travel about 100 times the distance of Earth from the Sun.

You would need to line up
31.64 million
Solar Systems in a row to equal the diameter of the Milky Way.

A cluster is a group of galaxies. Our Milky Way is in a cluster called the Local Group.

You would need to line up
100
Milky Way galaxies in a row to equal the diameter of the Local Group.

The Local Group is part of a bigger collection of galaxies called a supercluster – the Laniakea Supercluster.

You would need to line up
52
Local Groups in a row to equal the diameter of the Laniakea Supercluster.

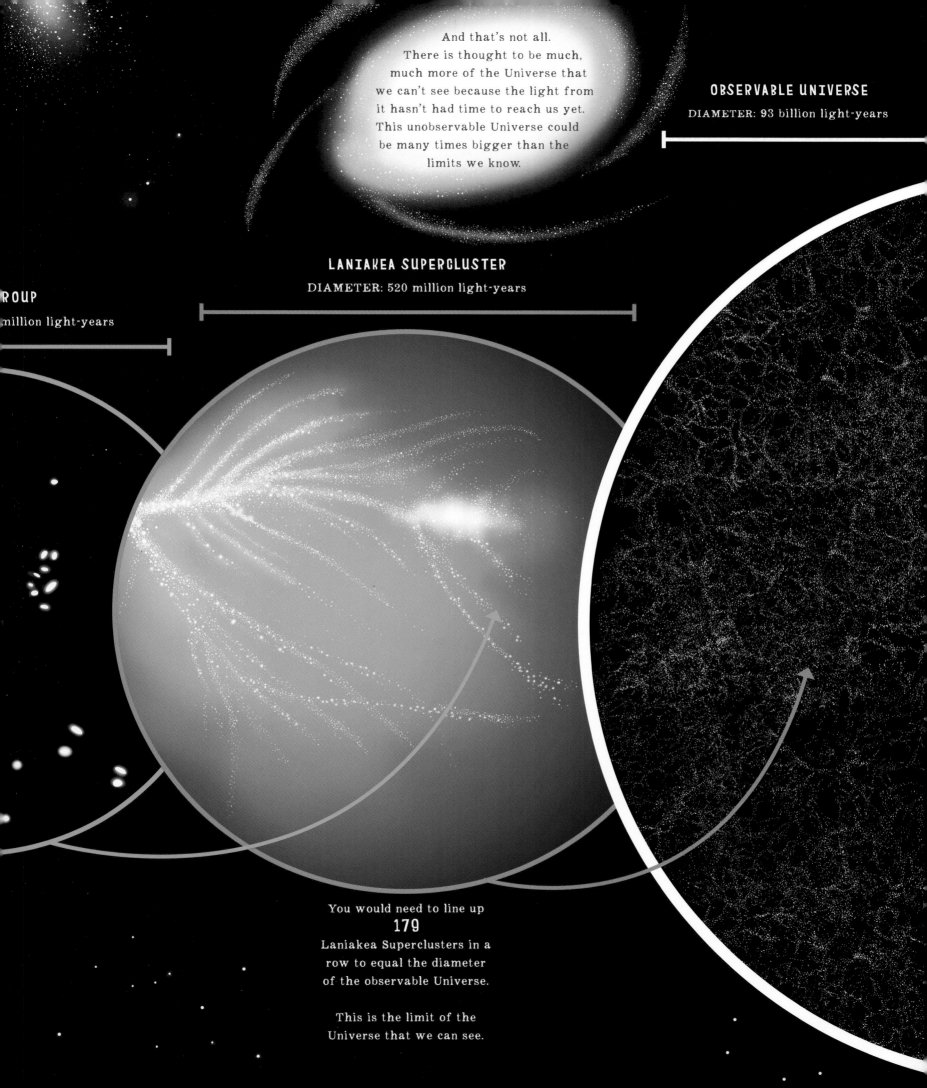

And that's not all.
There is thought to be much,
much more of the Universe that
we can't see because the light from
it hasn't had time to reach us yet.
This unobservable Universe could
be many times bigger than the
limits we know.

OBSERVABLE UNIVERSE
DIAMETER: 93 billion light-years

LANIAKEA SUPERCLUSTER
DIAMETER: 520 million light-years

ROUP
million light-years

You would need to line up
179
Laniakea Superclusters in a
row to equal the diameter
of the observable Universe.

This is the limit of the
Universe that we can see.

Gravity Greats

Gravity is an invisible force that pulls objects towards each other. Objects with more mass (more stuff in them) have more gravity. For example, the Sun's gravity is strong enough to keep all of the planets in the Solar System orbiting around it.

EARTH **MOON** **MARS**

DOWN!

The gravity of a star or planet pulls objects towards its centre. This is what makes things travel down to its surface. In only 10 seconds, an object can fall 490.33m to the surface of Earth.

Other bodies in space have different amounts of gravity. How far can objects fall in 10 seconds on these? The more gravity there is, the further an object will fall!

81.1m

186.1m

490.33m

00:10

UP!

The amount of gravity a star or planet has affects how far objects can travel up from its surface.

If you were a champion high jumper, how high could you leap on different bodies in space? The less gravity there is, the higher you would go!

On Earth, you might leap as high as **2m.**

There's only **16%** of Earth's gravity on the Moon, so you could leap **12m.**

There's less gravity on Mars than on Earth (just **37%**), so you could leap as high as **5.3m.**

Weight is a measure of the force of gravity between two particular objects — for example, you and Earth.

Because gravity varies on other objects in space, so would your weight. If you weighed 45kg on Earth, here's how it would change (rounded to the nearest half kilogram).

7.5kg
MOON

17kg
MARS

108kg
JUPITER

48.5kg
SATURN

1,260kg
SUN

JUPITER

SATURN

PLUTO

SUN

31m

541m

1,176m

6% of Earth's gravity on Pluto would send you soaring 31.7m!

More than twice Earth's gravity on Jupiter (236%) would restrict your jump to just 0.83m.

On Saturn, there's 107% of Earth's gravity, so you could leap 1.9m.

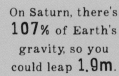

13,720m

On the Sun, you'd struggle to clear 7.16cm. Gravity here is 2798% that on Earth. That's around 28 times more.

BIG Bugs

Most creepy crawlies are small, but some, like the life-size creatures here, can grow surprisingly big!

Each wing is about the same width as a 9-year-old's hand.

QUEEN ALEXANDRA'S BIRDWING BUTTERFLY

From wingtip to wingtip, the female of this butterfly can measure up to **30cm**...

...in comparison, the Sinai baton blue is the world's smallest butterfly, with a wingspan of just **1cm**.

STICK INSECT

Found in China, the *Phryganistria chinensis Zhao* is the world's longest insect.

Its body is **36.5cm** long but it has an overall length of **62.4cm** when measured from forelegs to hindlegs...

...that's equal to eight large red admiral butterflies placed wingtip to wingtip.

x 8

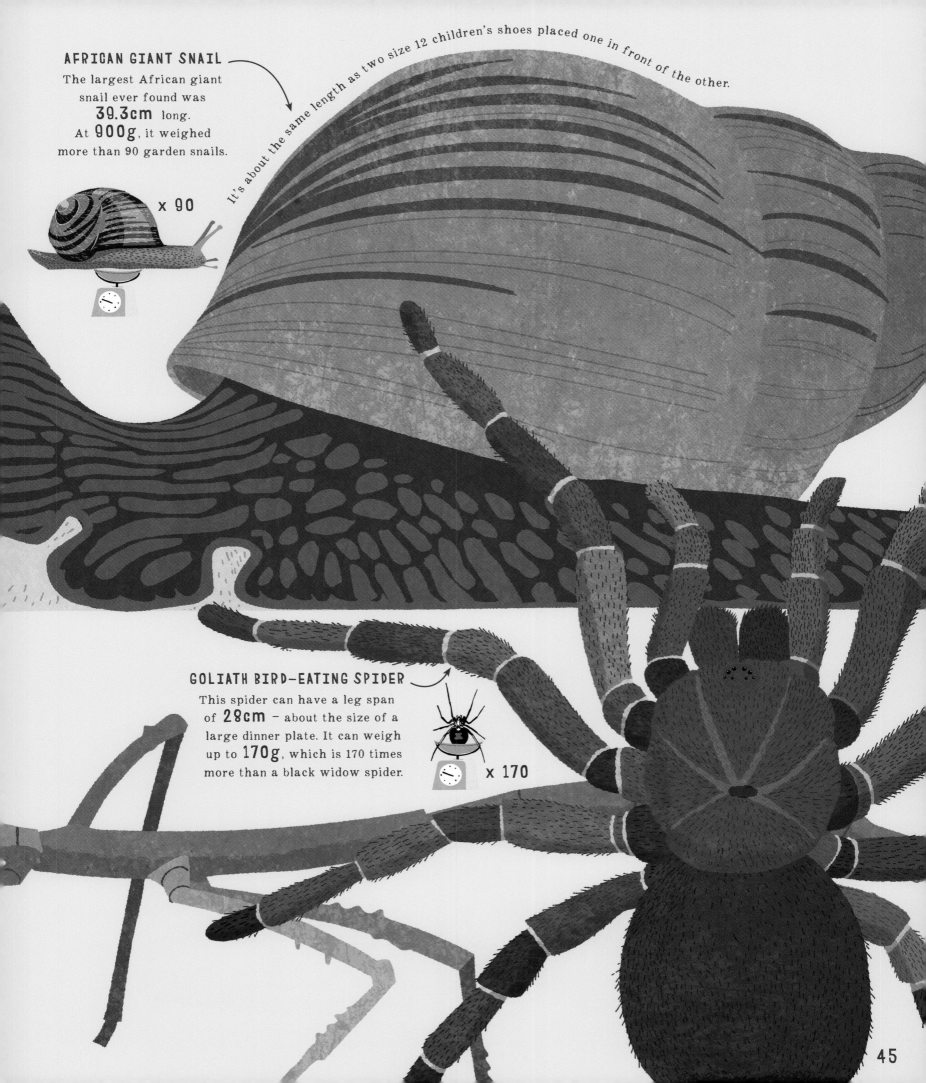

AFRICAN GIANT SNAIL

The largest African giant snail ever found was **39.3cm** long. At **900g**, it weighed more than 90 garden snails.

x 90

It's about the same length as two size 12 children's shoes placed one in front of the other.

GOLIATH BIRD-EATING SPIDER

This spider can have a leg span of **28cm** – about the size of a large dinner plate. It can weigh up to **170g**, which is 170 times more than a black widow spider.

x 170

45

Miniature Marvels

Earth's biggest creatures often hog the headlines, but small-scale animals deserve attention, too. These tiny species are all shown here life size.

PYGMY MOUSE LEMUR

The body of this little animal is up to **6.1cm** long. That's about the same size as a satsuma and smaller than an ordinary apple.

The lemur's tail can measure up to **13.6cm** – more than twice the length of its body.

This teeny lemur weighs around **30–40g**...

...a little less than a golf ball.

LITTLE PYGMY POSSUM

The head and body of this mini marsupial measure just **5–6.5cm** long.

One sitting on top of another would be shorter than a teaspoon!

At **6–8g**...

...the little pygmy possum weighs the same as two sugar cubes.

DWARF LANTERNSHARK

A fully grown adult male can measure just **16cm** long, which is shorter than a pencil.

The lanternshark's head takes up about a quarter of its entire length. Each jaw has 30 rows of tiny teeth.

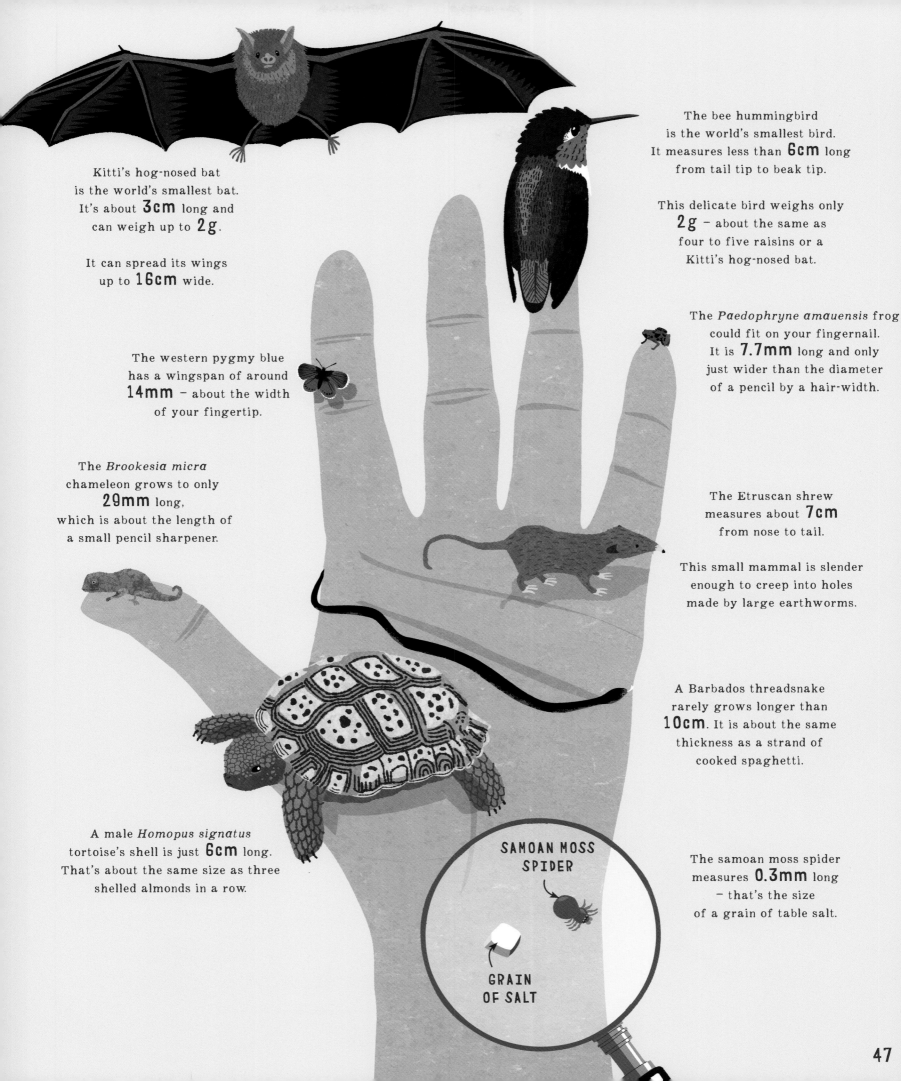

Kitti's hog-nosed bat is the world's smallest bat. It's about **3cm** long and can weigh up to **2g**.

It can spread its wings up to **16cm** wide.

The bee hummingbird is the world's smallest bird. It measures less than **6cm** long from tail tip to beak tip.

This delicate bird weighs only **2g** – about the same as four to five raisins or a Kitti's hog-nosed bat.

The western pygmy blue has a wingspan of around **14mm** – about the width of your fingertip.

The *Paedophryne amauensis* frog could fit on your fingernail. It is **7.7mm** long and only just wider than the diameter of a pencil by a hair-width.

The *Brookesia micra* chameleon grows to only **29mm** long, which is about the length of a small pencil sharpener.

The Etruscan shrew measures about **7cm** from nose to tail.

This small mammal is slender enough to creep into holes made by large earthworms.

A Barbados threadsnake rarely grows longer than **10cm**. It is about the same thickness as a strand of cooked spaghetti.

A male *Homopus signatus* tortoise's shell is just **6cm** long. That's about the same size as three shelled almonds in a row.

SAMOAN MOSS SPIDER

GRAIN OF SALT

The samoan moss spider measures **0.3mm** long – that's the size of a grain of table salt.

Microscopic

You might think the full stop at the end of this sentence is small. Think again! Many things on these pages are too small for the human eye alone to see.

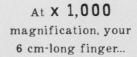

SEEING BIGGER

Small things can be viewed using an optical microscope, which uses glass lenses to magnify light. The most powerful optical microscopes can magnify things **1,000 times** or more.

At **x 1,000** magnification, your 6 cm-long finger...

...would loom at the gigantic size of **60m**, taller than the Leaning Tower of Pisa.

This almond nut, rice grain and grain of table salt are all **ACTUAL SIZE**

An average (shelled) almond is **21mm** long...

...3.5 times bigger than a **6mm** grain of rice, which is...

...20 times bigger than a **0.3mm** grain of table salt.

MALE PARASITIC WASP
0.14MM

A grain of salt is twice as big as the world's smallest insect. It would take **150** of these creatures in a row to equal the length of an almond.

Really tiny objects can be viewed using an electron microscope. This uses a beam of electrons instead of light to magnify the object up to **1–2 million** times its true size.

HUMAN SKIN CELL
30 MICROMETRES

A human skin cell is **4.66** times smaller than a male parasitic wasp. It takes billions of these cells to make up your skin, which is the largest organ in your body.

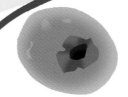

RED BLOOD CELL
7.5 MICROMETRES

A typical red blood cell is sixteen times smaller than a human skin cell. A row of around **11** red blood cells would span the diameter of a single human hair.

THE TINY MEASUREMENTS GUIDE

1 millimetre = 1,000 micrometres (um)

1 micrometre = 1,000 nanometres (nm)

1 nanometre = 1 billionth of a metre

SCALING UP

How small are some of the smallest things compared to an everyday object? Well, a golf ball is **4.27cm** in diameter – that's **42,700,000** nanometres.

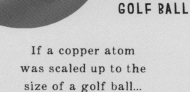

ACTUAL SIZE GOLF BALL

The golf ball is **5,693** times larger than a typical red blood cell. So if the blood cell was the size of a golf ball...

The golf ball is **427,000** times bigger than a flu virus. So, if the flu virus was the size of a golf ball...

If a copper atom was scaled up to the size of a golf ball...

...to be in scale, the golf ball would have to be **243m** tall; about three quarters the height of the Eiffel Tower!

...to be in scale, the ball would have to be **18,233m** tall: twice as tall as Mount Everest!

...the diameter of the ball would be **7,293km**, bigger than Mars!

FLU VIRUS
100 NANOMETRES

The flu virus is 25 times smaller than a *Salmonella typhi* bacteria.

DNA
2.5 NANOMETRES

A strand of human DNA is 40 times smaller than a flu virus. The chemical DNA contains all the information about how a living thing will look and behave.

SALMONELLA TYPHI BACTERIA
2,500 NANOMETRES

A typical *Salmonella typhi* bacteria is around three times smaller than a red blood cell. This bacteria is responsible for the infectious disease called typhoid fever.

COPPER ATOM
0.25 NANOMETRES

It would take 10 microscopic atoms of the chemical element copper laid side by side to equal the width of a strand of DNA.

It would take around **400,000** copper atoms to equal the thickness of this page.

LARGEST and Heaviest

Earth is big enough for a wide variety of seriously sized creatures to flourish. See just how large life can get in the natural world.

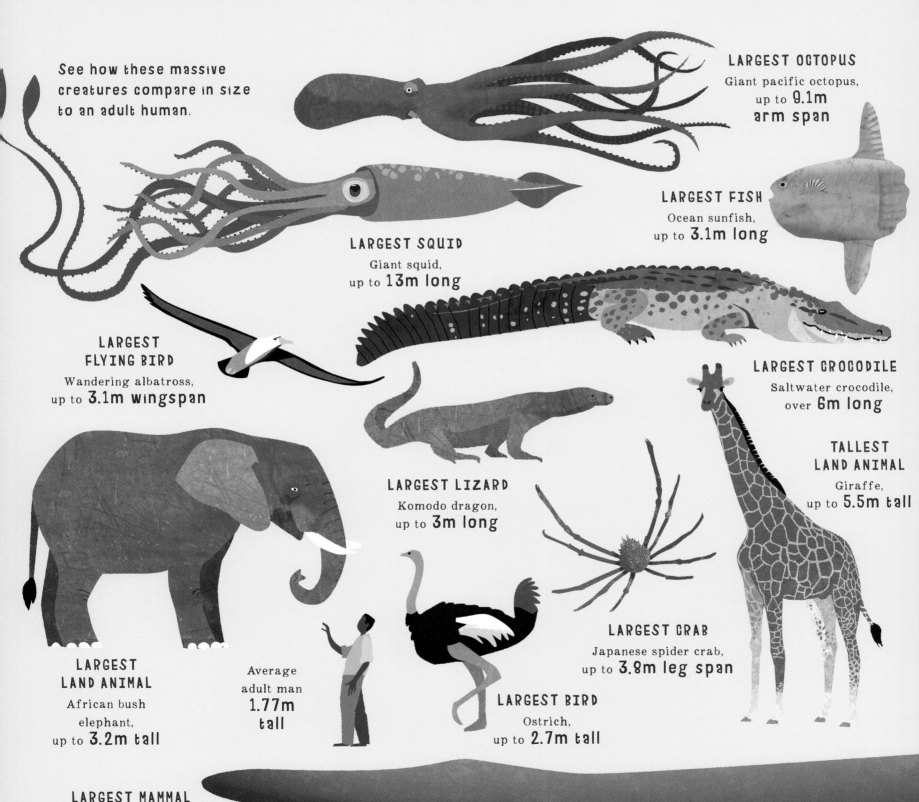

See how these massive creatures compare in size to an adult human.

LARGEST OCTOPUS
Giant pacific octopus, up to **9.1m** arm span

LARGEST SQUID
Giant squid, up to **13m** long

LARGEST FISH
Ocean sunfish, up to **3.1m** long

LARGEST FLYING BIRD
Wandering albatross, up to **3.1m** wingspan

LARGEST CROCODILE
Saltwater crocodile, over **6m** long

LARGEST LIZARD
Komodo dragon, up to **3m** long

TALLEST LAND ANIMAL
Giraffe, up to **5.5m** tall

LARGEST LAND ANIMAL
African bush elephant, up to **3.2m** tall

Average adult man **1.77m** tall

LARGEST BIRD
Ostrich, up to **2.7m** tall

LARGEST CRAB
Japanese spider crab, up to **3.8m** leg span

LARGEST MAMMAL
Blue whale, up to **29.9m** long

50

A WEIGHTY PROBLEM

How many different creatures does it take to equal the weight of a single blue whale? Follow the maths and see!

  =

1 x budgerigar 35g   **7 x budgerigars**   Approximately **1 x clownfish 250g**

  =   =

1 x Arctic hare 5kg   **5 x hedgehogs**   **1 x hedgehog 1kg**   **4 x clownfish**

 =   =

9 x Arctic hares   **1 x emu 45kg**   **6 x emus**   **1 x zebra 270kg**

 =   =

1 x African elephant 5,500kg   **5 x black rhinoceros**   **1 x black rhinoceros 1,100kg**   **4 x zebras at 275kg**

 =   +

5 x African elephants   **1 x humpback whale 27,500kg**   **5 x humpback whales**   **1 x large hippopotamus 4,500kg**

 =

1 x large Adult blue whale 142,000kg

The BIG One

When it comes to large living things, you don't get much bigger than the blue whale – it's a whopper! At up to 29.9 metres in length, it's roughly the length of the Boeing 737–100 jet airliner.

For something so big, the blue whale's eye is surprisingly small – about the size of a large grapefruit.

ACTUAL SIZE EYE

A blue whale's fleshy tongue weighs more than **2 tonnes**. It could easily fit two football teams plus substitutes and referees standing on it!

The blue whale's mouth can hold almost **100 tonnes** of saltwater. But its narrow throat stops it swallowing anything larger than a beach ball.

Adult blue whales can vary greatly in weight from 70 tonnes to giants weighing **190 tonnes**.

x 83

To balance that weight on a massive set of scales...

...would take 83 great white sharks!

The spray of air (and a little water) from the blowhole when the whale breathes out can rise more than **9m**...

...that's almost the height of a three-storey building!

WHALES ON SCALES

A baby blue whale measures approximately **7m** long...

...that's about the same length as a large motorhome.

They can weigh as much as **2,700kg**...

...that's about the same weight as a small full-grown adult hippopotamus!

Calves guzzle down their mother's milk. A calf can drink **379 litres** of milk per day...

...that's enough to fill **2.5** bathtubs.

An adult blue whale's heart...

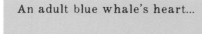

It weighs around **450kg**. Your heart weighs 300g at most.

...is the size of a small car.

A blue whale's two lungs can hold **5,000 litres** of air.

This amount would fill 455 11-litre size scuba tanks.

x 455

A blue whale's call can reach **188 decibels**...

...that's around 38 decibels louder than an aircraft's jet engine.

The low-pitched sounds can travel underwater for **800km**...

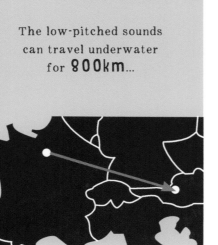

...that's about the same distance as travelling in a straight line from Paris, France, to Salzburg, Austria.

A blue whale's tail fins, called flukes, would fill a full-sized football goal.

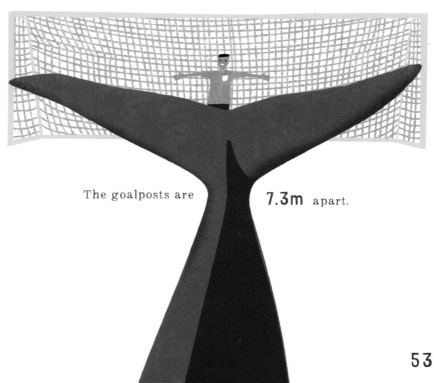

The goalposts are **7.3m** apart.

PREHISTORIC Proportions

For millions of years, reptiles like dinosaurs and pterosaurs existed on Earth. Some were surprisingly small, but many were MASSIVE!

PTERANODON

was a flying reptile with a wingspan of about 6.25m – that's almost the size of a hang-glider!

DIPLODOCUS

had an incredibly long neck and tail, giving it a length of around 26m, which is more than twice as long as a *Tyrannosaurus rex*.

ANKYLOSAURUS measured up to 7m long and was 1.7m tall at its hips – slightly shorter than a human.

MAN
1.77m TALL

MICROPACHYCEPHALOSAURUS

measured just 50–60cm long; roughly the size of a modern cat. It was found in China and is one of the smallest dinosaurs yet discovered.

VELOCIRAPTOR

was 1.8m long, but only 60–75cm tall – about waist-high to a human.

TYRANNOSAURUS REX

could reach 12.3m long and stood around 4.5–6m tall. It weighed around 7 tonnes – about the same as a male African elephant and four zebras.

The largest-known dinosaur footprints measure over 1.7m long – almost as tall as a full-grown man.

ARGENTINOSAURUS

HUMAN   TYRANNOSAURUS REX

ARGENTINOSAURUS
grew up to **37m** long – that's longer
than a row of three double-decker buses!

QUETZALCOATLUS
had a wingspan that stretched to **11m**,
which is bigger than the wingspan
of an F-16 jet fighter.

STEGOSAURUS
grew up to **9m** long and
weighed **3 tonnes**,
which is more than
four cows.

TRICERATOPS
measured up to **9m** long – the
same length as a row of **five**
velociraptors.

BIGGEST Poopers and Eaters

You don't have to be big to eat and poop a lot— but it helps! Here are some record-breaking poopers and eaters.

LENGTH IN METRES

| 0 | 1 | 2 | 3 | 4 | 5 | 6 | 7 | 8 | 9 | 10 | 11 | 12 | 13 |

Blue whales can eat as much as **3,600kg** of krill in a day.

Krill are 4–5cm long and weigh about 1g.

3,600kg is a typical weight for a small adult female African elephant.

The weight of the blue whale's tongue alone is roughly $^2/_3$ the weight of this elephant!

The blue whale's daily food intake is only... **2.5%** ...of their total body weight.

30 metres is the incredible length of their 'fecal plumes' (poop to you and me). That's almost the length of three buses!

EXTREME EATERS

MEANIES
Tear-drinking moths in Madagascar sneak up on larger animals and poke them in the eyes until they cry so they can drink the tears.

FASTEST EATER
The star-nosed mole is one of the fastest eaters. It eats its food in 227 milliseconds (less than a quarter of a second).

NAUGHTY CAECILIANS
Baby caecilians (earthworm-like amphibians) use temporary fangs to strip the skin from their mother's body and feast upon it.

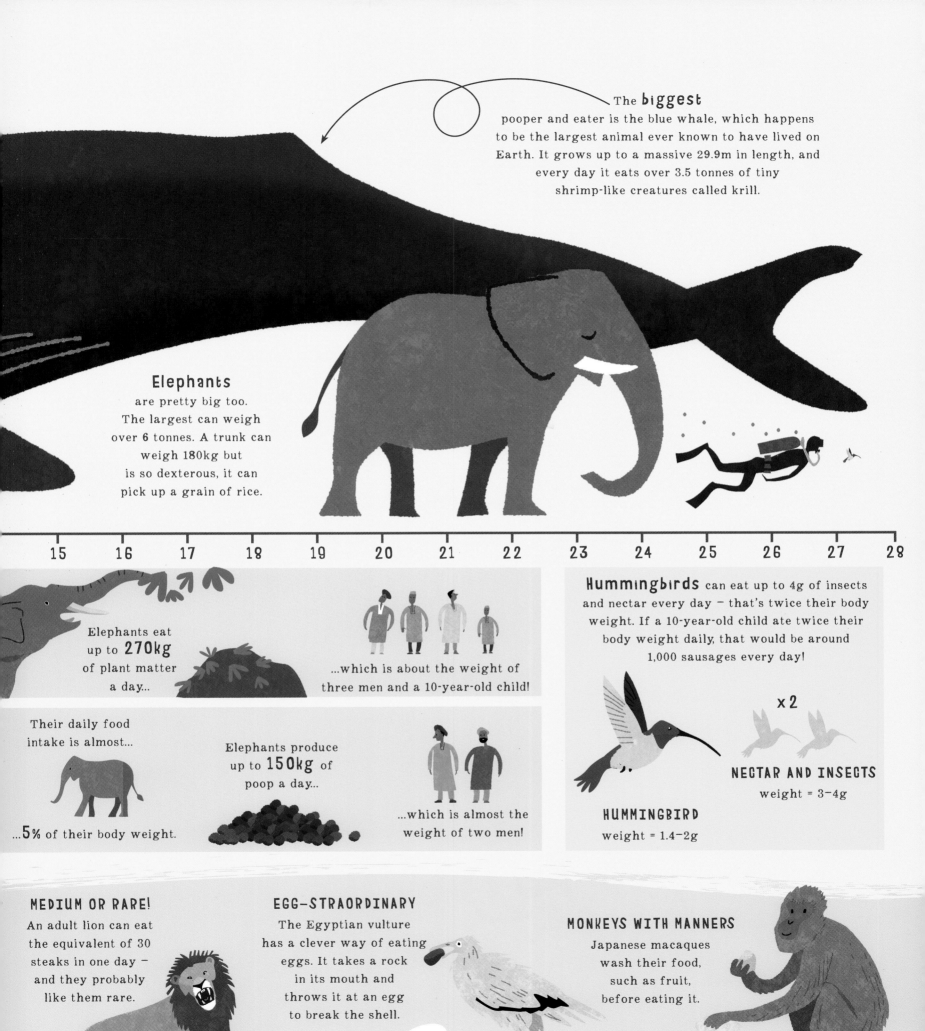

The **biggest** pooper and eater is the blue whale, which happens to be the largest animal ever known to have lived on Earth. It grows up to a massive 29.9m in length, and every day it eats over 3.5 tonnes of tiny shrimp-like creatures called krill.

Elephants

are pretty big too. The largest can weigh over **6** tonnes. A trunk can weigh 180kg but is so dexterous, it can pick up a grain of rice.

15 16 17 18 19 20 21 22 23 24 25 26 27 28

Elephants eat up to **270kg** of plant matter a day...

...which is about the weight of three men and a 10-year-old child!

Their daily food intake is almost...

...**5%** of their body weight.

Elephants produce up to **150kg** of poop a day...

...which is almost the weight of two men!

Hummingbirds can eat up to 4g of insects and nectar every day – that's twice their body weight. If a 10-year-old child ate twice their body weight daily, that would be around 1,000 sausages every day!

x 2

NECTAR AND INSECTS
weight = 3–4g

HUMMINGBIRD
weight = 1.4–2g

MEDIUM OR RARE!

An adult lion can eat the equivalent of 30 steaks in one day – and they probably like them rare.

EGG-STRAORDINARY

The Egyptian vulture has a clever way of eating eggs. It takes a rock in its mouth and throws it at an egg to break the shell.

MONKEYS WITH MANNERS

Japanese macaques wash their food, such as fruit, before eating it.

Daring and Dangerous

People take part in extreme sports for the challenge and the adrenalin rush. But with thrills can come spills. So, which sports are the most risky?

BE SAFE, HAVE FUN

All sports involve a level of risk and set out clear guidelines and safety measures to keep participants safe. If you want to try out a new sport, make sure you are with a responsible adult and understand the rules.

HANG-GLIDING

Flying without engine power, while hanging beneath a sail-like wing, can be deadly for an average 1 in every 116,000 flights in the UK.

PARKOUR

In this sport, people 'free run' through a built-up environment. They run, jump and clamber from place to place as they move around.

BASE JUMPING

Jumpers leap off cliffs, bridges, towers or skyscrapers, with next-to-no time to pull their parachute cord. Around 1 in 254 jumps end in injury and 1 in 2,317 in death.

BASE stands for Building, Antenna, Span (of a bridge) and Earth (such as a cliff).

CANOEING AND KAYAKING

Waterways are rated around the world from class 1 (gentle and relatively safe) to class VI (treacherous and potentially deadly). Overall, there is an estimated death rate from canoeing of 2 per 100,000 outings.

SCUBA DIVING

The aqualung allows divers to explore the ocean depths, but at a risk. There are roughly 140 deaths per year, worldwide, or 1 death every 200,000 dives.

DON'T TRY THIS AT HOME!

FREAKY FREEFALL

In 2014, Alan Eustace freefell from a height of 41.42km! He fell 37.6km in just 4 minutes, 27 seconds and reached 1,321kph before opening his parachute and landing safely.

IN REVERSE

A Dutch mountain biker, Pieter de Hart, cycled facing backwards over tough terrain in 2002. He travelled 50km in 2 hours, 8 seconds.

DEEP BREATH

Free divers hold their breath and dive as deep as they can. Some can hold a single breath for over 3½ minutes and descend more than 95m – the height of Big Ben's tower in London.

SKYDIVING

Jumping out of a plane and parachuting to the ground is both super-exciting and risky. In the USA in 2015, an average 6.1 jumps per million were fatal.

In 2014, a tandem skydive went dreadfully wrong when neither the main parachute or the back-up chute opened. A pair of skydivers fell over 4,200m, through the air — but survived!

EXTREME MOUNTAINEERING

High-altitude and hazardous routes, such as to the top of Mount Everest, can be risky. Over 290 climbers have lost their lives on Everest since the 1920s.

SKIING

In the 2015–16 ski season in the USA, over 52.8 million ski outings were taken altogether and 39 people perished, an average of 0.74 deaths per one million ski outings.

BUNGEE JUMPING

Diving down through the air with only a stretchy elastic cord to break your fall may be thrilling but carries some risk of death — about 1 in 500,000.

SNOWBOARDING

With lower speeds than skiing, snowboarders rarely risk death, but injuries are common. Wearing helmets and protective clothing reduces the risk of serious head injury by about 40%.

MOTOCROSS RACING

Even with body armour and helmets, racing over rough terrain and performing stunts on motocross bikes carries serious risks of injury.

MOTOR RACING

Race cars can reach over 321kph as they zoom round the track. Although crashes often happen, few are deadly.

HUMAN HAMSTER BALL

In zorbing, a person is harnessed inside a giant, see-through plastic ball and can roll downhill faster than 45kph — the same speed as a top 100-m male sprinter.

EXTREME IRONING

The aim of this sport is to iron clothes in unlikely places! In 2006, British scuba diver Louise Trewavas set up a weighted ironing board at a depth of 137m under the Red Sea — and ironed a T-shirt.

BRRR!

Wim 'Iceman' Hof scaled the snowy peak of Mount Kilimanjaro in 2009 wearing nothing but his shorts. He has also immersed himself completely in ice for 1 hour, 52 minutes.

Sizing Up Sport

Did you know you could fit 104 table tennis tables into a single NBA basketball court? Or that the men's world triple jump record is just 1cm shorter than the length of three boxing rings in a row*? When it comes to comparing in sport, it can be a numbers game.

SPEEDY SPORTS

77.25KPH **Rugby union** The fastest timed pass was made by Joe Simpson of the English club, Wasps, in 2011.

100KPH **Javelin** An elite male athlete sends a javelin soaring away at this speed.

116KPH **Table tennis** This record table tennis ball speed came off the bat of Polish player, Łukasz Budner in 2016.

161.3KPH **Cricket** The fastest measured cricket ball bowled was by Shoaib Akhtar for Pakistan versus England in a 2003 match.

169.14KPH **Baseball pitch** The fastest Major League Baseball pitch was thrown by the Cincinnati Reds' Aroldis Chapman in 2010.

177.5KPH **Ice hockey** Denis Kulyash recorded this super-fast shot during a Continental Hockey League competition in Russia in 2011.

183KPH **Football** The fastest football was struck by David Hirst in an English Premier League game in 1996.

240KPH+ **Archery** An Olympic archer's arrows fly 70m to their target at speeds of over 240kph.

An archery arrow can fly twice as fast as a cheetah can sprint.

263KPH **Tennis** Sam Groth struck tennis's fastest-ever serve during the 2012 Busan Open.

The average speed of the fastest-ever lap in Formula 1 was 0.8kph slower than the fastest-ever tennis serve.

332KPH **Badminton smash** Fu Haifeng hit this shot during the 2005 Sudirman Cup.

This super-fast badminton shuttlecock travelled seven and a half times faster than the top speed of champion sprinter Usain Bolt!

349.38KPH **Golf drive** A golf ball reached this incredible speed after a shot by Ryan Winther in 2012.

*At the time of going to press – new world records are made all the time!

SPORTING HIGH-LIGHTS

See the heights some athletes can reach!

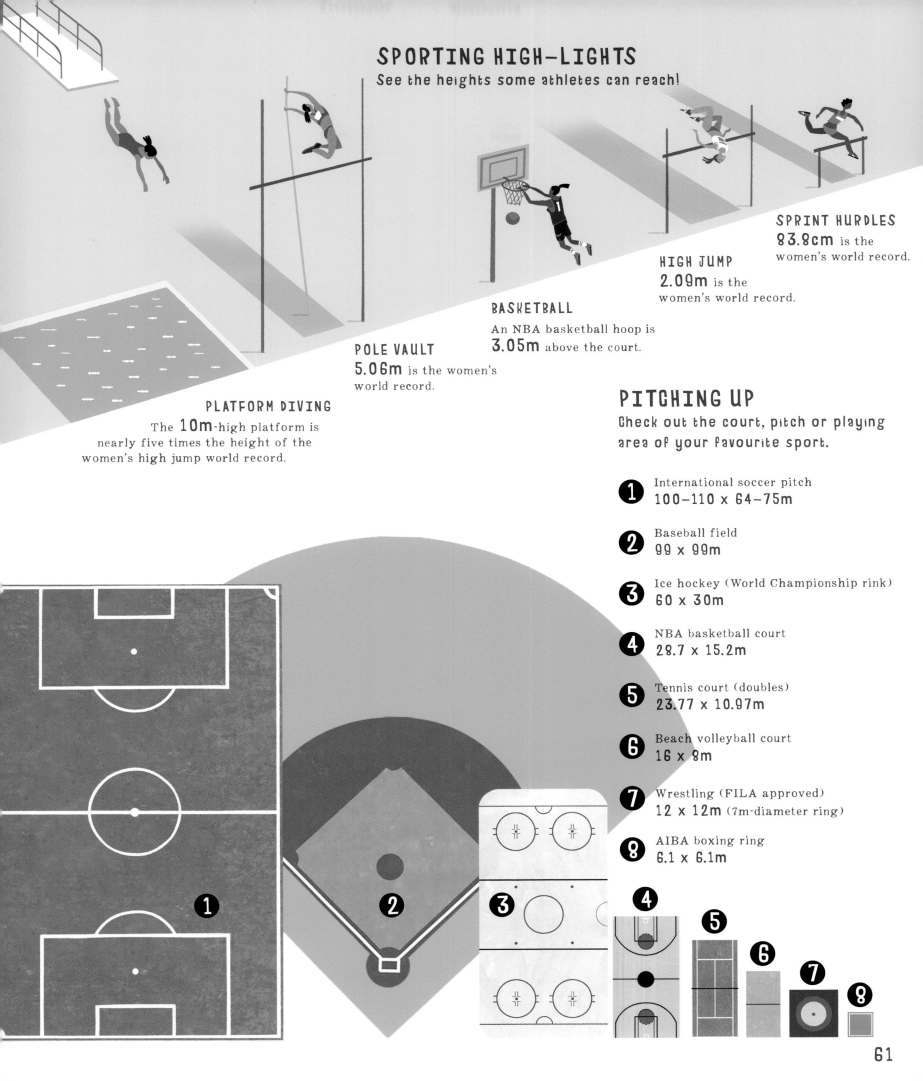

SPRINT HURDLES
83.8cm is the women's world record.

HIGH JUMP
2.09m is the women's world record.

BASKETBALL
An NBA basketball hoop is **3.05m** above the court.

POLE VAULT
5.06m is the women's world record.

PLATFORM DIVING
The **10m**-high platform is nearly five times the height of the women's high jump world record.

PITCHING UP

Check out the court, pitch or playing area of your favourite sport.

1. International soccer pitch
   100–110 x 64–75m

2. Baseball field
   99 x 99m

3. Ice hockey (World Championship rink)
   60 x 30m

4. NBA basketball court
   28.7 x 15.2m

5. Tennis court (doubles)
   23.77 x 10.97m

6. Beach volleyball court
   16 x 8m

7. Wrestling (FILA approved)
   12 x 12m (7m-diameter ring)

8. AIBA boxing ring
   6.1 x 6.1m

JUMP!

Humans are great at jumping, but we've got strong competition from the long-distance leapers of the animal world.

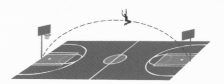

Grasshopper
1m

1m	2m

Grasshoppers and kangaroo rats may not be able to jump as far as humans can but, for their size, they're the real superstar long jumpers! Both animals can jump approximately **20 times** their body length, which is equal to an adult man clearing a basketball court in a single standing jump.

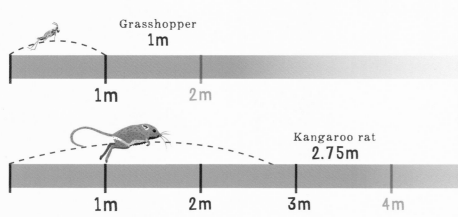

Kangaroo rat
2.75m

1m	**2m**	**3m**	4m

With the help of a run up before taking off, top male athletes can jump up to **five times** their body length.

Women's long jump world record
7.52m

1m	**2m**	**3m**	**4m**	**5m**	**6m**	**7m**	**8m**

Even from a standing start, a kangaroo can out-jump an Olympic long jumper. Its powerful rear legs propel it through the air at a speed of 5m per second.

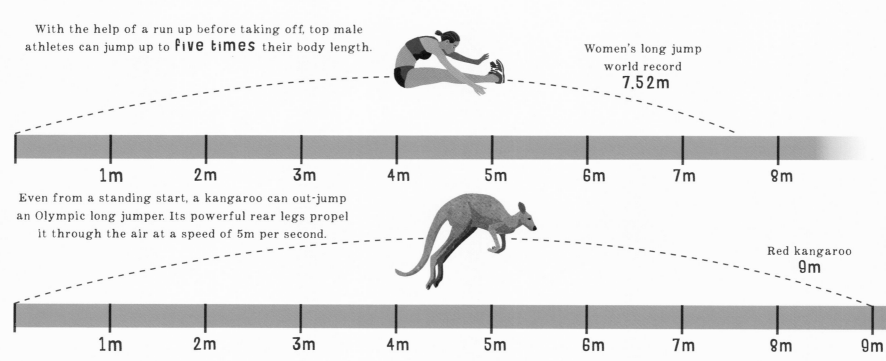

Red kangaroo
9m

1m	**2m**	**3m**	**4m**	**5m**	**6m**	**7m**	**8m**	**9m**

READY, SET, GO!

POWER JUMP

Fleas can jump 200 times their own body length. Dog fleas jump higher than cat fleas. Both are beaten by an undersea animal called a copepod that can accelerate to a speed of 1,000 body lengths per second when it jumps.

A LONG WAY...

At 76.8m, the length of the farthest-ever discus throw by a female athlete is slightly shorter than a row of seven double-decker buses.

FLYING LEAP

Several species of flying frogs use large webbed feet to glide up to 15m between trees.

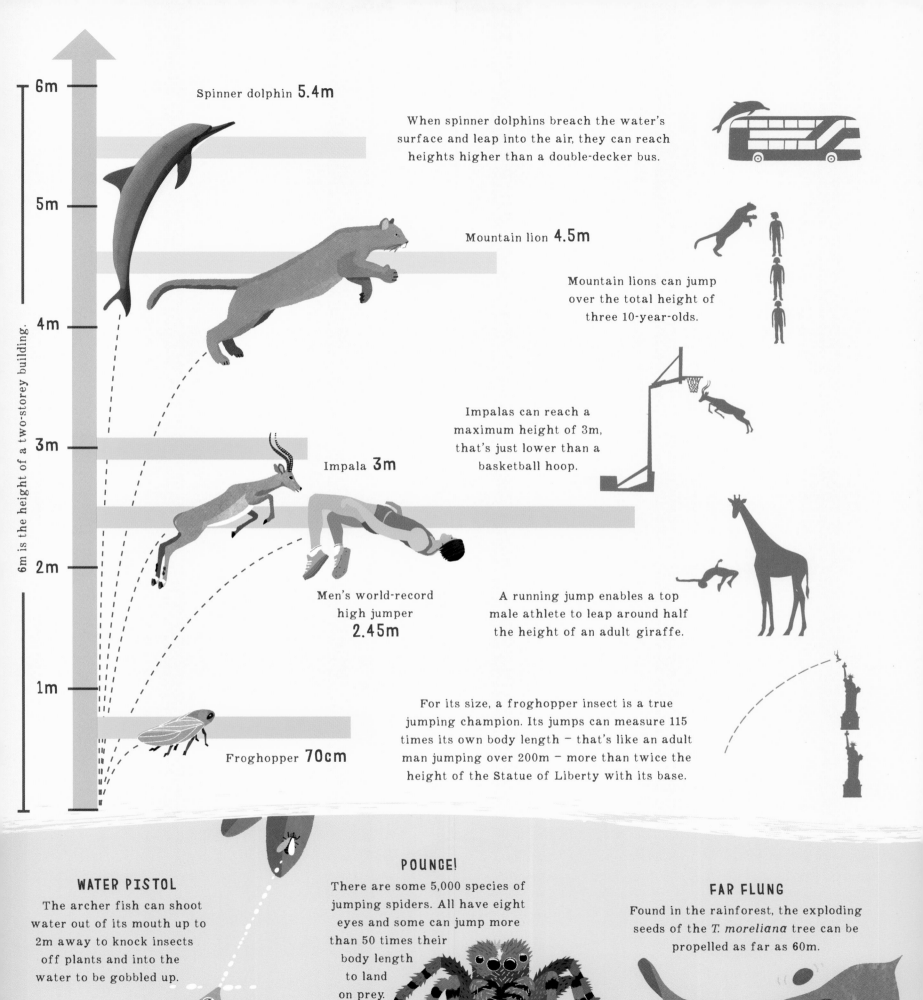

6m is the height of a two-storey building.

Spinner dolphin **5.4m**

When spinner dolphins breach the water's surface and leap into the air, they can reach heights higher than a double-decker bus.

Mountain lion **4.5m**

Mountain lions can jump over the total height of three 10-year-olds.

Impalas can reach a maximum height of 3m, that's just lower than a basketball hoop.

Impala **3m**

Men's world-record high jumper **2.45m**

A running jump enables a top male athlete to leap around half the height of an adult giraffe.

For its size, a froghopper insect is a true jumping champion. Its jumps can measure 115 times its own body length – that's like an adult man jumping over 200m – more than twice the height of the Statue of Liberty with its base.

Froghopper **70cm**

WATER PISTOL

The archer fish can shoot water out of its mouth up to 2m away to knock insects off plants and into the water to be gobbled up.

POUNCE!

There are some 5,000 species of jumping spiders. All have eight eyes and some can jump more than 50 times their body length to land on prey.

FAR FLUNG

Found in the rainforest, the exploding seeds of the *T. moreliana* tree can be propelled as far as 60m.

Speed Champions

In a race, humans would be slower than many animals. The fastest creatures are built for speed — it helps them to catch prey and to escape from their enemies.

AIR

The top animal speeds are in the air. The fastest bird, the peregrine falcon, can outstrip some light aircraft when swooping for prey.

Housefly **7.2kph**

Little brown bat **35.4kph**

Dragonfly **58kph**

Anna's hummingbird **98kph**

LAND

Some land animals are either sprinters or marathon runners. Like horses, humans can run for long distances at a steady pace.

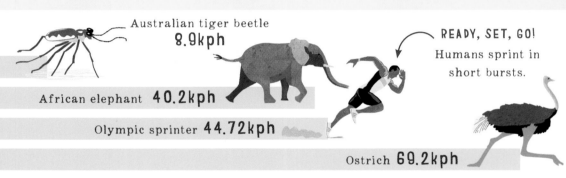

Australian tiger beetle **8.9kph**

African elephant **40.2kph**

Olympic sprinter **44.72kph**

READY, SET, GO! Humans sprint in short bursts.

Ostrich **69.2kph**

Pronghorn antelope **88.5kph**

WATER

Human speeds can be timed but measuring how fast animals move is trickier, especially in water.

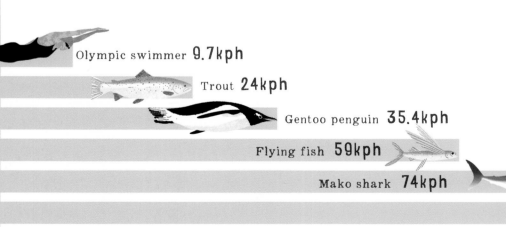

Olympic swimmer **9.7kph**

Trout **24kph**

Gentoo penguin **35.4kph**

Flying fish **59kph**

Mako shark **74kph**

kph   10   20   30   40   50   60   70   80

We measure speeds in kph (kilometres per hour). These measurements tell us the distance covered by a person, animal or vehicle in one hour.

COUNTING BODY LENGTH

At around 7cm long (not including the bill), Anna's hummingbird can fly 385 times its body length each second – faster than a space shuttle re-entering Earth's atmosphere.

8kph
The American woodcock has the lowest recorded flying speed of any bird, going just a tiny bit faster than a housefly.

VS

389.5kph
Over three times swifter than a cheetah, the peregrine falcon is the world's speediest animal! It flies fastest when diving to capture its prey in mid-air.

Racing pigeon **145kph**

Golden eagle **193kph**

Peregrine falcon **389.5kph**

CAT POWER

The top sprint speed of a domestic cat is 46.7kph, beating the human world record of almost 45kph by a whisker.

0.048kph
The speed at which the slowpoke snail creeps along is around 100 times slower than the average human walking pace.

VS

112.7kph
A cheetah accelerates from 0 to 112.7kph in just three seconds – that's at the same rate as a Porsche or a Ferrari supercar.

Cheetah **112.7kph**

DENSITY DRAG

Water density is over 750 times greater than air density. This means that record-breaking speeds in water take a lot of effort, so the fastest swimmers are the biggest, strongest animals.

0.0014kph
The dwarf seahorse is the world's slowest fish. It takes it over two hours just to swim 3 metres!

VS

128.7kph
For a long time, the sailfish was thought to be the world's fastest fish. Then a black marlin was recorded swimming at 128.7kph! That's 16kph faster than a cheetah and over 13 times the speed of our fastest human swimmers.

Black marlin **128.7kph**

| 100 | 110 | 120 | 130 | 140 | 150 | 160 | 170 | 180 | 190 | 200 |

Speed machines

You've seen the planet's speediest creatures; now meet its most rapid machines and compare the speeds they can reach on land, sea and in the air.

Human-powered aircraft (Musculair 2)
44.26kph

Airship (Zeppelin LZ N07-100)
115kph

Glider (Schempp-Hirth Nimbus-4) **306.8kph**

Helicopter (Westland Lynx AH.1) **400.89kp**

AIR

Tank (S2000 Scorpion Peacekeeper) **82.23kph**

Steam train (A4 Mallard) **202.5km/h**

Land yacht (Ecotricity Greenbird) **203.1kph**

This land yacht races along smooth beaches, salt flats or frozen lakes powered only by the wind catching its carbon fibre sail.

LAND

Sailing ship (*Cutty Sark*)
32.4kph

Cruise ship (MS *Harmony of the Seas*) **46kph**

The record-breaking *Jenny II* hovercraft was powered by a car engine.
Hovercraft (*Jenny II*)
137.4kph

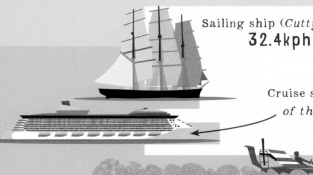

Waterskier Fernando Reina Iglesias from Mexico (towed by a helicopter)
246.2kph

WATER

| | 50 | 100 | 150 | 200 | 250 | 300 | 350 | 400 | 450 |

kph

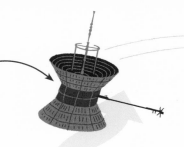

Launched into space by powerful rockets, the Helios II space probe reached a top speed of 246,960kph. At that rate, it could travel from Los Angeles to New York in 57.5 seconds and complete a round-the-world journey in under 10 minutes!

10.9kph
The speed of the first successful heavier-than-air plane, the Wright Flyer, on its maiden flight in 1903.

VS

7,270kph
The fastest-ever manned aircraft, the rocket-powered North American X-15A-2 in 1967.

Civilian jet plane
(Cessna Citation X+)
978kph

Spy jet plane (SR71A Blackbird) **3,529.56kph**

Rocket (Helios II space probe) **246,960kph**

Train (SC Maglev L0)
603kph

20.1kph
The maximum speed of a Segway.

VS

431.07kph
The top speed of the world's fastest mass-produced car, the Bugatti Veyron Super Sport.

Shockwave's three jet engines generate around 460 times the power of a small car.

Truck (Shockwave)
605kph

Jet car: the Thrust SSC is the world speed record holder. Powered by two jet engines, it raced from 0–960kph in just 16 seconds and used 18.18 litres of fuel every second! **1,227.99kph**.

9.3kph
The top speed of the fastest pedal-powered boat, which is slower than many people can jog.

VS

244.94kph
The record speed of an F1 3-litre powerboat raced by Guido Cappellini in 2005; this is faster than most cars.

Powerboat
(*Spirit of Australia*)
511kph

550   600   650   700   750   800   850   900   950   1,000   1,050

Stre-e-e-tch

Vehicles vary in size from mini bikes to massive trains and ships. Let's see how some of the world's lengthiest vehicles measure up.

An average car is usually between **4.1m** and **4.6m** long.

A Chevrolet Suburban SUV is **5.7m** long.

That's about the same length as three people lying head to toe, and only 70cm shorter than the first successful aircraft, the 6.4m-long Wright Flyer 1, which made its first flight in 1903.

The AutoTram Extra Grand bus in Germany measures over **30m** and can carry up to 256 passengers...

...that's around the same length as a blue whale, and around 2m shorter than HMS *Endeavour*, the ship Captain James Cook and 93 others sailed in from England to Australia in 1769.

This Australian road train measures **53.5m** and is a series of trailers pulled by a single, powerful truck...

...which is about as long as four giant squid, laid end-to-end.

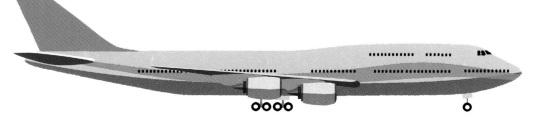

At **76.3m**, the longest airliner in the world is the Boeing 747-8...

...that's around the same length as three whole tenpin bowling lanes (and their approaches).

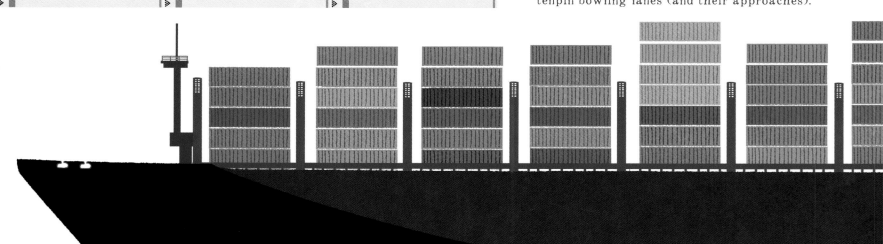

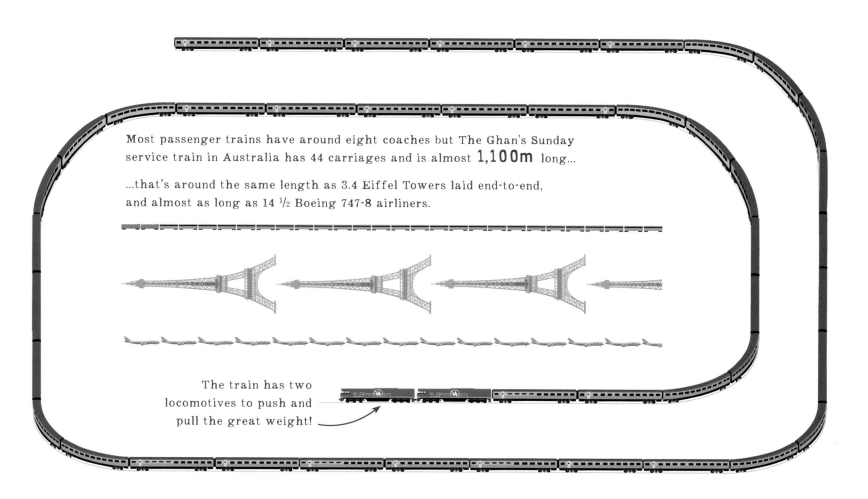

Most passenger trains have around eight coaches but The Ghan's Sunday service train in Australia has 44 carriages and is almost **1,100m** long...

...that's around the same length as 3.4 Eiffel Towers laid end-to-end, and almost as long as 14 ½ Boeing 747-8 airliners.

The train has two locomotives to push and pull the great weight!

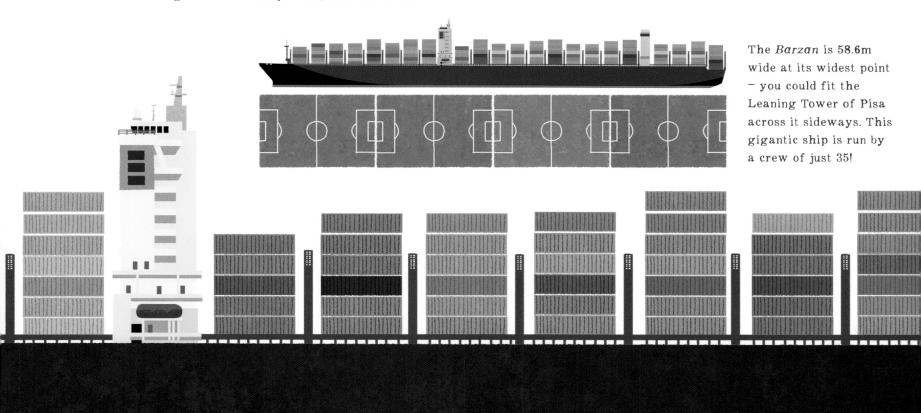

At **400m** long, the *Barzan* is a container ship of extreme length! It's about as long as four soccer pitches, laid end-to-end.

The *Barzan* is 58.6m wide at its widest point – you could fit the Leaning Tower of Pisa across it sideways. This gigantic ship is run by a crew of just 35!

Space Racers

Check out and compare six of the most amazing and momentous machines to have left Earth and explored space.

INTERNATIONAL SPACE STATION (ISS)

Assembled in space during more than 100 missions, and still being added to, this giant space station houses crews of six astronauts who perform hundreds of scientific experiments.

At **109m** long by **73m** wide...

...the ISS is about the same size as a full-sized soccer pitch.

Although it appears weightless in space, it actually has a mass of **419,725kg**...

x15

...about the weight of 15 humpback whales.

The ISS orbits Earth at a speed of over **28,000kph**...

x8

...almost eight times faster than the world's fastest jet plane, the SR71A Blackbird.

APOLLO 11 LUNAR MODULE

The first spacecraft to carry humans to the Moon, it reached the lunar surface in 1969.

Loaded with two astronauts and fuel, it weighed **15,103kg**...

...that's heavier than two *Tyrannosaurus rex* dinosaurs plus three large tigers.

The **9.4m**-wide spacecraft stood **7m** tall...

...about the height of two African elephants.

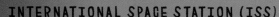

ENDEAVOUR ORBITER

One of five NASA space shuttles, the Endeavour Orbiter flew 25 missions in space between 1992 and 2011 when it was retired.

The spacecraft weighed **78,000kg** empty...

 x14

...as much as 14 African elephants.

At **37.2m** long...

...it was about the same length as an Airbus A320 airliner.

United States — *Endeavour*

SATURN V

This mega-powerful launch vehicle carried Apollo spacecraft to the Moon (1969-73).

At **111m** high, it stood almost twice as high as the Leaning Tower of Pisa.

Full of fuel, the rocket weighed **2.84 million kg** at lift-off...

 x103

...that's about as much as 103 humpback whales.

SPUTNIK 1

The first-ever space satellite was launched in 1957 and spent three months orbiting Earth at a speed of around **29,000kph**.

On Earth, the satellite weighed **83.6kg** – about the weight of a large red kangaroo.

The satellite was a **58cm**-wide metal ball...

...about the size of a beach ball.

CURIOSITY ROVER

Landing on Mars in 2012, the six-wheeled Curiosity rover has been exploring the Red Planet ever since.

Its top speed on Mars is a slow **0.14kph** – not much faster than the average sloth.

The rover weighs **899kg**...

...the same as three large tigers.

At **2.7m** long and **2.2m** wide...

...it is roughly the size of a small car.

MEGA Machines

Humans are quite strong for their size, but also smart enough to build powerful machines to do their lifting, pushing and digging. Here are some of the mightiest.

Telescope boom

The largest mobile crane in the world is called the Liebherr LTM 11200-9.1. It can lift weights of up to **1,200** tonnes... ...that's more than the weight of eight blue whales.

The crane has a boom that telescopes inwards so that the 19.95m-long vehicle can drive from site to site. The boom then extends outwards when the crane needs to lift things high – it can stretch up to **100m** high, which is about as high as a 28-floor building, and with attachments can go even taller.

The world's largest dump truck is called the BelAZ 75710. Its total weight when fully loaded is **810** tonnes, which is roughly **six** houses!

Unloaded, it weighs **360** tonnes, which is the same as **two and a half** blue whales.

x 6

Each wheel is **4m** high... ...that's nearly two and a half times as tall as an average woman.

One of the biggest tunnel-boring machines in the world is called Bertha.
It grinds away rock and soil like a giant drill bit to create tunnels and pipelines.
Its large motor produces **25,000** horsepower...
...that's more power than 16 monster trucks.

 x 16

Its cutting head uses
260 steel teeth
to cut a **17.4m**
diameter hole
through rock and soil.

The tunnel it
creates is as tall as
three adult
giraffes.

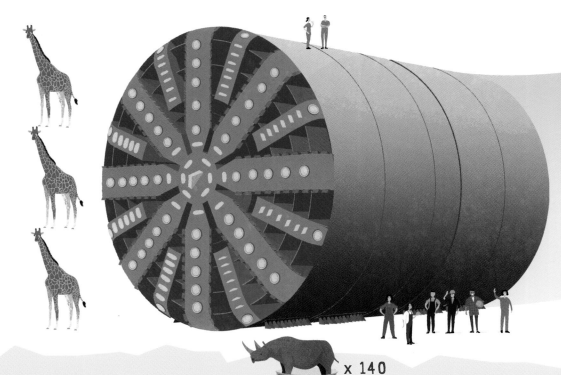

x 140

A giant bulldozer, called the Komatsu
D575A-3 SD, weighs over **152 tonnes**...

...that's about the same weight as
140 black rhinoceros.

The huge blade is almost
twice the height of
an average man...

...and more than
the length of
the longest-ever
reticulated
python.

The blade can lift up to
69 cubic metres
of material in one go...

x 445

...that's enough to fill
over **445** bathtubs
full of rock and dirt.

Magnifiers and magnets

Not all huge machines are about physical force. Meet two devices that use electricity, mirrors and magnets to perform incredible feats.

The Very Large Telescope (VLT) is a huge space observatory high in the Atacama Desert in Chile. It gathers in light and uses giant mirrors to focus and magnify images it receives from outer space.

The VLT is **2,635m** above sea level — that's more than three times the height of Burj Khalifa, the world's tallest building.

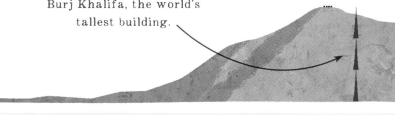

Each telescope has a giant mirror that weighs **23** tonnes...

...that's almost as much as two double-decker buses.

=

The VLT is actually four large telescopes.

Each telescope weighs **430** tonnes...

...that's almost as heavy as a fully loaded Boeing 747 jumbo jet.

Each mirror measures **8.2m** in diameter.

This distance is roughly equal to five women, standing one on top of the other.

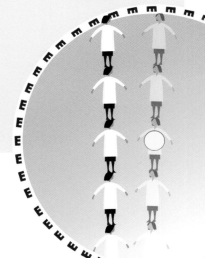

When the four telescopes work together, the VLT's magnifying power is amazing.

It can view objects up to **4 billion** times fainter than you can see.

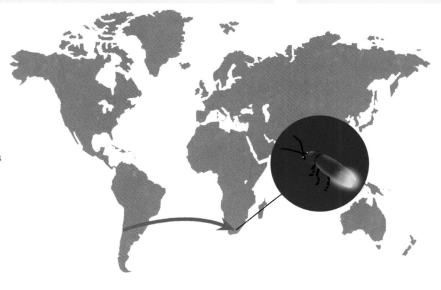

For example, it could spot a 10mm-long firefly insect up to **10,000km** away, which would be like the telescope in Chile viewing the insect in Johannesburg in South Africa.

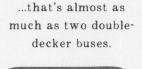

The Large Hadron Collider (LHC) is a giant underground tunnel that crosses the border between France and Switzerland. It's the world's biggest physics experiment, involving some of the world's tiniest things! The tunnel is lined with thousands of powerful magnets and electric fields that push and pull tiny particles, called protons. The protons race both ways around the LHC tunnel and crash into each other. Scientific instruments measure what happens during these collisions and scientists use this information to explore and understand more about the whole structure of space and time!

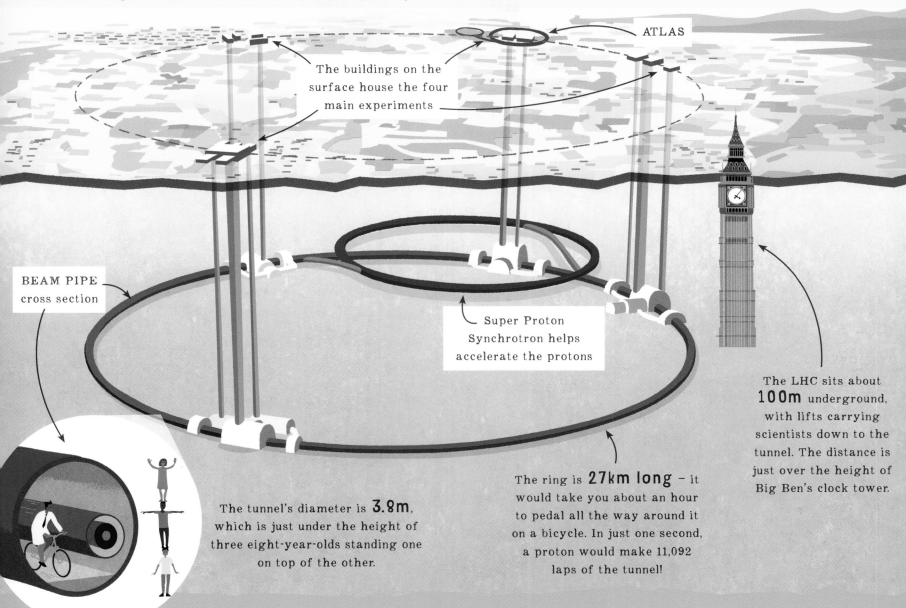

The buildings on the surface house the four main experiments

ATLAS

Super Proton Synchrotron helps accelerate the protons

BEAM PIPE cross section

The LHC sits about **100m** underground, with lifts carrying scientists down to the tunnel. The distance is just over the height of Big Ben's clock tower.

The tunnel's diameter is **3.8m**, which is just under the height of three eight-year-olds standing one on top of the other.

The ring is **27km long** – it would take you about an hour to pedal all the way around it on a bicycle. In just one second, a proton would make 11,092 laps of the tunnel!

Protons are tiny particles that are found inside atoms. An atom is about one tenth and a proton is about **one millionth** of a **nanometre**. (And a nanometre is about one billionth of a metre!)

If a proton was the size of a marble...

...the atom it is part of would be about as big as a small town.

ATLAS is one of the LHC's four huge scientific instruments that measures what happens when the proton beams collide.

ATLAS is as tall as...

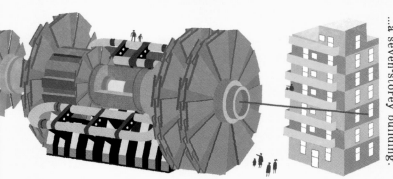

...a seven-storey building.

Strongest Animals

You can probably lift some pretty heavy things, from a 4kg bag of potatoes to a heavy piece of wood. Even so, the average human actually looks puny compared to the weightlifters of the natural world.

HUMANS

This adult man weighs **80kg**.

He can lift **one and a quarter** times his own body's weight.

 = **100kg**

100kg is the weight of five fully packed suitcases (according to the baggage allowance for most airlines). Many people can lift only their bodyweight or less. A few can lift more.

AFRICAN CROWNED EAGLES

These large, powerful birds of prey feed on monkeys and small mammals. They can lift prey weighing as much as **four** times their own bodyweight...

...that's equal to our man lifting about eight emus.

GORILLAS

Their super-strong arms, legs and chest enable them to lift up to **10** times their bodyweight...

...that's equal to our man lifting about the same weight as a Formula 1 car and two sets of spare tyres!

LEAF-CUTTER ANTS

These ants cut and carry bits of leaf to their nests, which they turn into compost to grow food. They can lift up to **50** times their bodyweight...

...that's equal to our man lifting an adult rhinoceros and a large family car at the same time!

FEEL THE FORCE

BRUTAL BITE

When a saltwater crocodile bites, it can clamp down with as much as 16,460 Newtons of pressure – that's more than three and a half times more powerful than the bites of lions and tigers.

GRIPPING STUFF

The coconut crab has a seriously strong grip – up to 3,000 Newtons, which is 10 times the gripping power of the human hand.

TRAP THIEF

A wolverine is only the size of a medium dog, but powerful enough to open steel hunting traps with their jaws and haul away the captive animals inside.

3rd

RHINOCEROS BEETLES

are bulked-up beetles with a curved horn on their head. They can lift **100** times their own body weight...

...that's equal to our man lifting one big African elephant and a medium-sized white rhinoceros.

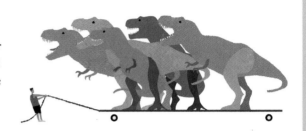

2nd

ORIBATID MITES

measure only 0.2mm long and weigh a tenth of a milligram. They can pull an impressive **530** times their own weight...

...that's equal to our man pulling around five *Tyrannosaurus rex* dinosaurs.

1st

THE STRONGEST HORNED DUNG BEETLES

have been measured pulling weights that are **1,141** times their own body weight...

...that's equivalent to our man pulling **91,280kg**, which is more than the weight of a Boeing 757-200 airliner.

ELEPHANTS

When it comes to strength relative to body weight, the biggest aren't always the strongest.

Elephants can lift **300kg** with their powerful trunks...

...but this is only around a 20th of their body weight. If humans could only lift a 20th of their bodyweight...

...it would take two 80-kg men to lift a dachshund!

PUSH-UP KING

Male lava lizards in the Galapagos Islands perform push-ups as a show of strength and to warn rival males away from their territory.

SILKY STRONG

The Chilean recluse spider spins silk threads made of lots of little loops. These make the silk up to five times stronger than steel!

WRAP STAR

An anaconda snake suffocates prey like deer or a cow by wrapping its long coils around them and squeezing hard.

Deadly Animals

Venomous creatures attack by injecting toxins into a victim, while poisonous animals are harmful if touched or eaten. Other living things can bite you, squash you or infect you with lethal diseases. Nice!

BOX JELLYFISH

Each of this jellyfish's tentacles are covered in stingers that inject venom.

A single tentacle can grow up to **4.6m**... ...about as long as a large car.

Just 3m of a single tentacle wrapped around a person can sting enough to kill.

BLUE-RINGED OCTOPUS

Up to **20cm** in size...

...an adult blue-ringed octopus can contain enough venom to kill...

...**26** humans in minutes.

KING COBRA

The longest venomous snake grows up to **5.5m**, which is as long as a pick-up truck.

500 milligrams of cobra venom is enough to kill an elephant or up to 20 people.

GOLDEN POISON DART FROG

The biggest are just **5.5cm** long, which is about the length of your little finger.

Their skin is covered in a poisonous sweat...

...enough to kill **10** people.

INLAND TAIPAN

One bite of this snake contains enough deadly venom to kill up to **100 people**...

...almost enough to fill an Airbus A318 airliner.

POWERFUL POISON AND TOXIC TENTACLES

PREY PARALYSER

The North American gila lizard oozes poison from glands in its lower jaw when it bites. This seeps into its prey's wounds, paralyzing it.

SNAPPY MOVER

Moving at up to 20kph, the black mamba is the world's fastest venomous snake. Its toxic bite can kill a person in just 30 minutes.

WHAT A RIP OFF!

The Portuguese man o'war uses its toxic tentacles to paralyse fish. The blanket octopus rips off the man o'war's tentacles to make its own lethal weapon.

ANIMAL ATTACKS

Meet the deadliest creatures in the world, and the approximate number of human deaths they cause per year (dpy). They're not always the ones you might expect!

Some species have larvae that can move out of the intestine to other organs of the body, sometimes leading to death.

TAPEWORM
2,000 DPY

TSETSE FLY
10,000

People are killed by bites which spread deadly sleeping sickness.

ASCARIS ROUND WORM
2,500 DPY

Living mostly in the intestines, these worms can cause deadly blockages in the body, especially the lungs.

MOSQUITO
725,000 DPY

Some species of female mosquitoes transmit malaria to humans, through a parasite. This first affects the liver and then enters the bloodstream, travelling around the body to other organs, sometimes causing them to fail.

ELEPHANTS
100 DPY

CROCODILE
1,000 DPY

SNAKES
50,000 DPY

Big size does not always mean a bigger threat. Among the most common causes of deadly snakebites in Asia are saw-scaled vipers, which can be just 30cm long.

DOGS
25,000 DPY

The majority of dog-related deaths happen when people are infected by rabies after contact with an infected dog.

HIPPOPOTAMUS
500 DPY

LIONS
100 DPY

WOLVES
10 DPY

SHARKS
10 DPY

HOODED HORROR

The hooded pitohui, from Papua New Guinea, eats toxic melyrid beetles. These don't kill the bird, but make its feathers poisonous, paralyzing any creatures that consume it.

LETHAL LORIS

The slow loris has a deadly secret! It sucks poison from a small patch on its elbow, mixes it with saliva and can deliver a painful, toxic bite to an enemy.

RAT POISON

The African crested rat gives itself a protective, venomous coat. It does this by chewing the bark from the poison arrow tree, then smearing its hair and fur with the toxic saliva.

Super senses

Senses gather information about sights, sounds, smells, tastes and sensations. But some animal senses can easily outsmart human ones.

SIGHT

Eyes are our sight organs. They gather in light from our surroundings and turn it into electrical nerve signals which the brain then interprets as images.

A human eye is about **2.4cm** in diameter...

ACTUAL SIZE HUMAN EYE

...which is around two-thirds the size of a ping-pong ball.

A colossal squid's eyeball is about **27cm** in diameter...

...slightly bigger than a basketball.

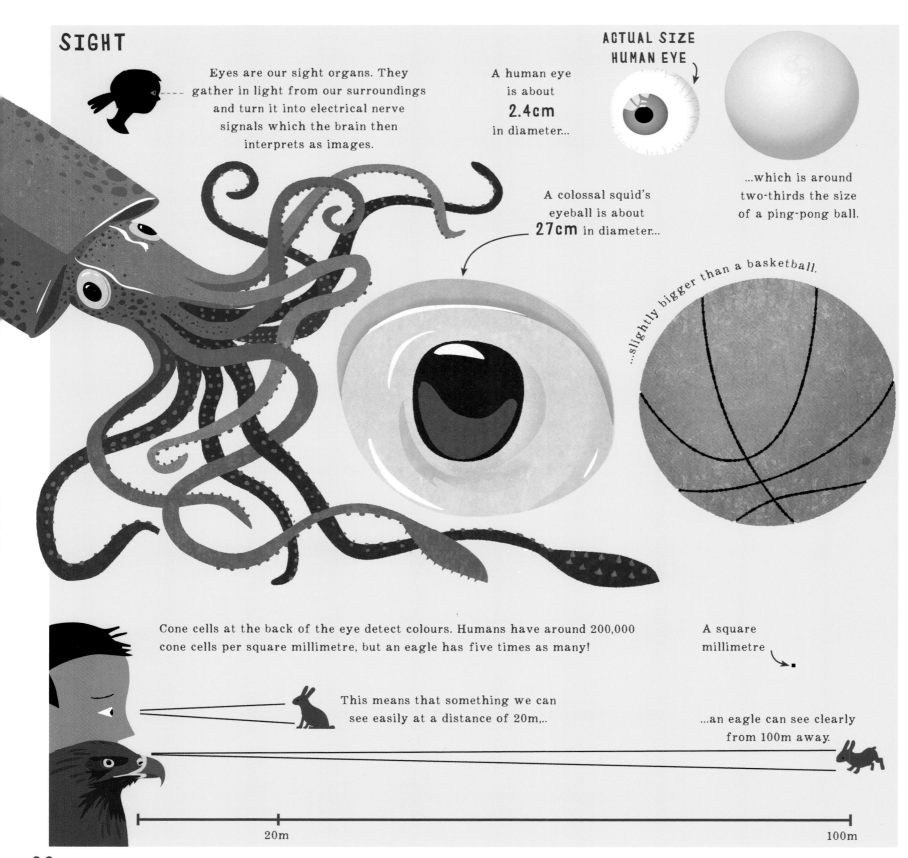

Cone cells at the back of the eye detect colours. Humans have around 200,000 cone cells per square millimetre, but an eagle has five times as many!

A square millimetre

This means that something we can see easily at a distance of 20m,..

...an eagle can see clearly from 100m away.

20m   100m

SOUND

Our ears collect sound waves moving through the air.
These waves are measured in Hertz (Hz).

Low Hz numbers mean low sounds...   ...and high Hz numbers mean high sounds.

0Hz	100	1,000	10,000	100,000

**Human hearing range
20-20,000Hz**

Human ears hear sounds as deep and low
as 20Hz and as high pitched as 20,000Hz.

**Cat hearing range
45-64,000Hz**

Cats can move their ears 180° and hear sounds more
than three times the upper limit of human hearing.

**Elephant hearing range
16-12,000Hz**

Elephants can make and hear sounds lower
than human hearing, known as infrasound.

SMELL

High up in your nose are millions of olfactory receptors.
These cells can detect as many as a trillion different smells.

There are
5-6 million
olfactory receptors
in a human nose.

VS

There are
220-300 million
olfactory receptors in a bloodhound's nose.
Its sense of smell is at least 1,000 times
stronger than a human's sense of smell.

A bloodhound can follow a single scent trail for **208km**,
even through crowded places containing many other smells.

TASTE

Taste buds are the sense organs on your tongue
that tell you if something is good to eat or not.

There are
2,000-8,000
taste buds on a
human tongue.

VS

250,000 taste buds
covering a catfish's entire body!

The catfish uses its taste buds to hunt
for prey in dark, muddy waters.

TOUCH

Your skin has over 200
touch receptors per
square centimetre. These
minute sense organs
detect pressure, pain,
heat or cold. The star-
nosed mole has 27,174
receptors per square cm
on it nose alone.

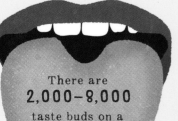

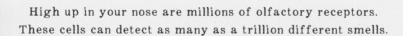

Survival stories

Most of us have easy access to food, water and shelter, but some creatures can survive in the most extreme conditions. Meet some of them here.

LEAST THIRSTY

The kangaroo rat is one mammal that can survive its entire lifetime without ever taking a direct drink of water. Instead, this small desert critter is able to survive solely on the moisture inside the desert plants that it eats.

MOST FLOOD-RESISTANT

When floods threaten a colony of fire ants, they are able to survive by quickly linking legs to form a densely-packed living life raft. Thousands of ants, packed together can float and survive for several weeks on the water.

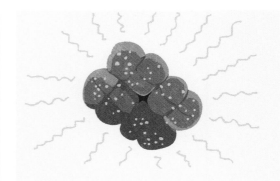

MOST RADIATION RESISTANT

The bacteria, *Deinococcus radiodurans*, can repair its own DNA after suffering extreme radiation. It's only 0.003mm in size yet can survive 1,000 times more radiation than an adult human.

TARDIGRADES

Tardigrades (also known as water bears) are an incredibly hardy water-dwelling species. Whatever you throw at these little critters, 1.5mm long at most, they seem to be able to handle it.

COLD
They can survive temperatures lower than -200°C – over ten times lower than inside a household freezer.

SPACE
In 2007, tardigrades were taken up into space and left there for 10 days without air to breathe. Many survived!

HEAT
Tardigrades have been known to survive 151°C – that's one and a half times the boiling point of water.

DRY
A tardigrade can dry out into a tiny husk and survive without water for more than 10 years. Humans can rarely make it through a week. Don't try! When rehydrated, tardigrades are right as rain!

PRESSURE
Researchers believe that tardigrades can withstand pressures six times that found at the bottom of the deepest oceans.

HOW DO HUMANS COMPARE

PHENOMENAL FALL
In 1944, rear gunner Nicholas Alkemade leapt from his flaming Lancaster bomber, without a parachute, preferring death by impact than burning. He fell a distance of 5,500m – around 17 Eiffel Towers – and landed in just 45cm deep snow yet survived with no broken bones. His speed before impact had been slowed by crashing through tree branches.

'HIBERNATING' HUMAN
Mitsutaka Uchikoshi survived for 24 days without food on the slopes of Mount Rokko in Japan after falling and breaking his pelvis. He was found with almost no pulse and his body temperature just 22°C (normal human body temperature is around 37°C). Astonishingly, scientists believed his body had shut down to protect him, a little like animals hibernate, and he made a full recovery.

FOOD... AT LAST!

Many creatures, including gnus, shrews – and you – like to eat each and every day. But some can go without food for long periods and still survive.

SHREW

Many species of shrew can only go a **few hours** without food before they die.

YOU

Humans can usually survive 35–40 days without food. Water, however, is a different story. Few can last more than **3–5 days** without it.

BED BUG

The common bed bug lives off human blood. but they can go without, yet still survive for **60–90 days.**

CAMEL

The humps on a camel's back aren't full of water but fat – as much as 40kg of it. This helps camels survive long periods without food – **60 days** is possible. The humps shrink and droop as the fat is used up.

EMPEROR PENGUIN

Left to look after their egg on Antarctica while their female mate dives into the ocean to feed, male emperor penguins can go **120 days** without food, during which time they lose as much as 40% of their body weight.

HUMPBACK WHALES

These giant whales consume up to 1,360kg of plankton, krill and small fish a day. They feed for around 120 days in cold ocean waters but migrate to warmer seas to breed where they may not eat for as long as **120–180 days**.

POLAR BEARS

A pregnant polar bear mother can go **120–240 days** without food after she gives birth and nurtures her cubs in a snow den. She relies on her reserves of fat to survive.

AFRICAN ROCK PYTHON

Many snakes can go months without food. The African rock python can survive for **over a year** without eating if its last meal was substantial enough. These large snakes are on average 3–5m long. They swallow hyenas, monkeys and even small crocodiles whole!

OLM (PROTEUS ANGUINUS)

This strange type of salamander lives in dark caves in eastern Europe. It typically grows about as long as a ruler (30cm) and can survive without food for **10 years.**

AFRICAN LUNGFISH

In times of drought, the African lungfish burrows into the bottom of a dry lake and goes into a hibernation-like state, not needing food or water for up to **five years**. It only wakes up when fresh water returns.

CROCODILES

Like snakes and many other cold-blooded creatures, crocodiles can slow their bodies down to survive many months without food. Individual crocodiles have been observed going an incredible **two years** without a meal.

MOUNTAIN ORDEAL

Lost in the Himalayas mountain range during the winter of 1992, Australian climber, James Scott survived 43 days on his own. Most of the time was spent under a rock ledge where he lived off just melted snow, two chocolate bars and a caterpillar he found!

WHALE SAVES WOMAN

Chinese female diver Yang Yun was taking part in a diving competition in 2009 when the cripplingly cold waters in the giant aquarium tank caused her legs to cramp and she couldn't swim to the surface. The tank's other resident, Mila, a beluga whale, grabbed her legs and helped the paralyzed diver to safety.

Growing UP

Living things develop, are born and grow up into adults in different ways and at different rates.

The gestation period is the time spent by a developing mammal inside its mother before it is born.

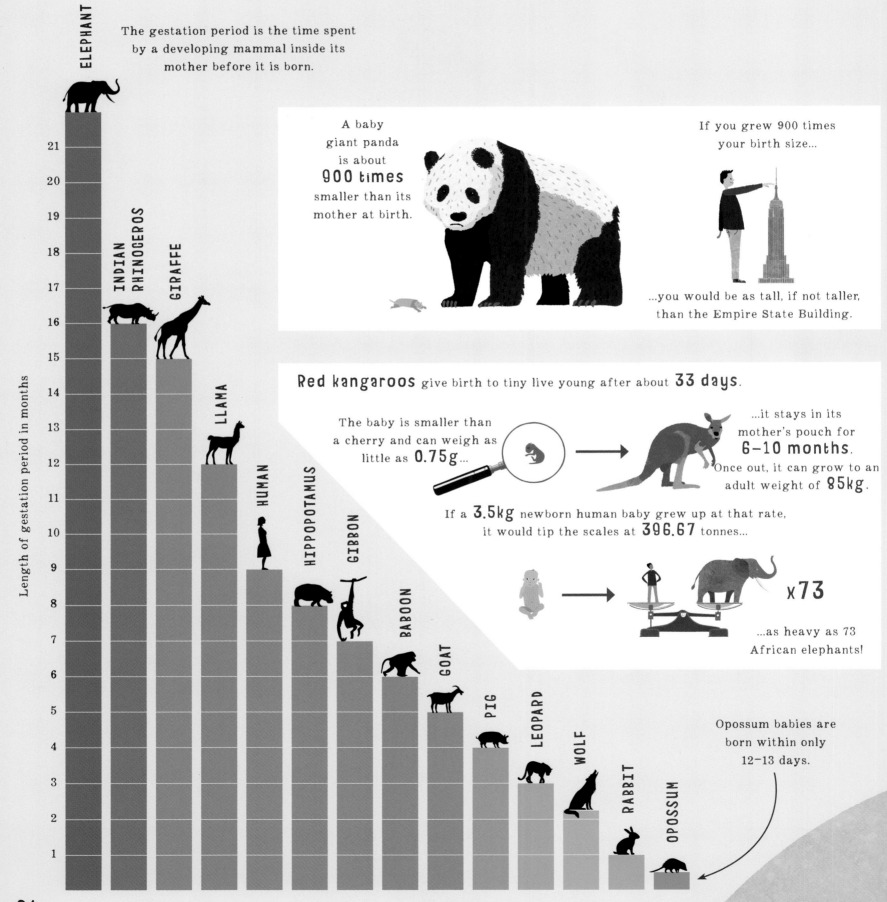

Length of gestation period in months

ELEPHANT

INDIAN RHINOCEROS

GIRAFFE

LLAMA

HUMAN

HIPPOPOTAMUS

GIBBON

BABOON

GOAT

PIG

LEOPARD

WOLF

RABBIT

OPOSSUM

A baby giant panda is about **900 times** smaller than its mother at birth.

If you grew 900 times your birth size... ...you would be as tall, if not taller, than the Empire State Building.

Red kangaroos give birth to tiny live young after about **33 days**.

The baby is smaller than a cherry and can weigh as little as **0.75g**...

...it stays in its mother's pouch for **6–10 months**. Once out, it can grow to an adult weight of **85kg**.

If a **3.5kg** newborn human baby grew up at that rate, it would tip the scales at **396.67** tonnes...

x73

...as heavy as 73 African elephants!

Opossum babies are born within only 12–13 days.

A human baby takes up to **180 days** to double its birthweight.

A horse foal doubles its weight in **60 days** – three times faster than a human baby!

A common seal baby can double its weight in **28 days**...

...and a rabbit in just **six days!**

If a **3.5kg** human baby kept on doubling its weight at the same rate as a rabbit...

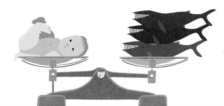

...after **three months, 12 days**, it would weigh more than three blue whales!

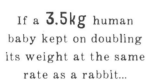

Fast growers also exist in the plant kingdom. **Giant kelp**, the largest type of seaweed, can grow up to **53m** – half the length of a **soccer pitch**.

Giant kelp can grow at a rate of up to **60cm** a day. If you grew at that rate...

...you would be **taller** than the world's tallest tree in **six and a half** months!

Humans have the longest childhood of almost any known creature (except Greenland sharks). They only become adults after puberty in their **teen** years.

Orangutans come second to humans. They depend on their parents for the first **eight years**.

Some species of killifish become adult and able to reproduce after only **17 days**.

Megapode birds fend for themselves straight away. They begin flying as soon as **24 hours** after hatching.

ELEPHANT BIRD
390 x 326mm
The biggest-ever bird's eggs came from a giant bird from Madagascar, which died out in the 17th century. One egg weighed more than **12kg** and could have made about **100** omelettes!

OSTRICH
150 x 130mm
A single egg can weigh over **1.4kg** – that's about the same as **28** small chicken eggs.

SIZING UP

Many creatures develop inside an egg, but they vary enormously in size. Take a look...

BEE HUMMINGBIRD
6.35 x 3mm long

BLUE TIT
16 x 12mm

EUROPEAN ROBIN
20 x 15.5mm

TEXAS TORTOISE
41.5 x 34mm

LOGGERHEAD TURTLE
41 x 41mm
A turtle mum can lay over 100 eggs in one go.

CHICKEN (MEDIUM)
55 x 40–48mm

CANADA GOOSE
86 x 58mm

Immortals

Life on Earth is diverse and life spans vary just as much. Meet some of the creatures and plants that live the shortest and longest lives of all.

400 YEARS

Greenland sharks can live to at least 272 years (and possibly to 500 years!). They don't reproduce until they're around 150 years old.

SPEEDY CRESS

The Thale cress plant lives for no longer than **5–7 weeks.** In that time it can grow up to 30–40cm tall and produce 10,000 seeds.

Jeanne Calment was the oldest confirmed person in the world. She died in 1997, but was born in 1875! She reached an age of 122 years and 164 days.

2–2.5 YEARS

Syrian hamsters are among our favourite pets.

9–12 MONTHS

The common shrew has the shortest lifespan in the wild of any group of mammals.

4–5 DAYS

Some gastrotrichs can go from egg to adult in three days. They die a day or two later.

71.5 YEARS

This is the global average lifespan of a person born in 2015.

A tuatara, named Henry, resident of the Southland Museum and Art Gallery in New Zealand, celebrated his 120th birthday in 2017.

24 HOURS

The mayfly has the shortest adult life of any known creature.

60+ YEARS

60 is the average lifespan of a tuatara, though some can live far longer.

100–200 DAYS

The German cockroach doesn't live very long, but it's so tough that it can survive up to a week without its head.

60–70 YEARS

Asian elephants normally live this long.

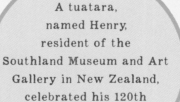

50–60 YEARS

Wild pink cockatoos are a type of parrot.

VINE TIME

The oldest known grape vine, in Slovenia, is **400–500 years** old. It still produces about 35–55kg of grapes each year.

PENSIONER PINE

A bristlecone pine in California, USA, was **5,067 years** old in 2017 and still growing! The tree was a seedling at the time of the early ancient Egyptians.

TWIN LEAVES

The welwitschia grows in the Namib Desert and, although it looks like a tangled heap, in fact, it has only two leaves. Some of these plants are believed to be over **1,500 years** old.

100 YEARS

Giant tortoises typically live to around 100 years, but some have been known to live to nearly 200.

In 2017, a giant tortoise, nicknamed Jonathan, was estimated to be 185 years old. Jonathan had been shipped from the Seychelles to the island of St Helena in the Atlantic in 1882 and lived there ever since!

500+ YEARS

Clams can live for a very long time.

One ocean quahog, nicknamed Ming, was gathered off Iceland in 2006, but killed when scientists placed it in a deep freezer in its 507th year alive. Ming was born in 1499, 10 years before Henry VIII became king of England.

4–5 MONTHS

The labord's chameleon spends 8–9 months as an egg but only survives 4–5 months as an adult before dying.

150 YEARS

Bowhead whales are the longest living of all whales.

A bowhead whale was found in 2007 with a 19th-century harpoon point in its body. Another whale found by scientists was thought to be 211 years old.

35–40 YEARS

This is the average life span of a wild gorilla.

IMMORTAL

Turritopsis dohrnii is a type of tiny jellyfish with an unusual lifecycle. It starts life as a larva and then anchors itself to the sea floor as a polyp, before becoming an adult jellyfish. It can also reverse the process – changing back from adult to polyp many times. This means it never really dies.

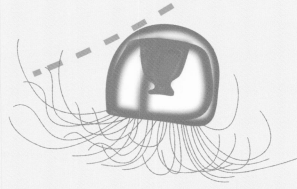

4,265 YEARS

Leiopathes sp. is a genus of black coral living thousands of metres deep in the ocean. In 2009, tests showed that a sample from close to the Hawaiian islands was more than 4,000 years old.

Earth's History IN A YEAR

Earth's history stretches back 4.550 BILLION YEARS, Such a huge amount of time is impossible to imagine. This is what it would look like squeezed into a single year.

JANUARY 1
4.55 billion years ago

Earth forms as the force of gravity pulls dust and gas together. The new planet orbits a new star, **the Sun**.

JANUARY 7
4.47 billion years ago

Earth's satellite, **the Moon**, forms.

Single-celled life forms appear.

MARCH 26
3.5 billion years ago

Storms of **asteroids and comets** stop bombarding Earth.

MARCH 2
3.8 billion years ago

JUNE 22
2.4 billion years ago

Large amounts of **oxygen** enter Earth's atmosphere.

Earth becomes a giant snowball in an **Ice Age** lasting nearly 300 million years.

JULY 16
2.1 billion years ago

AUGUST 1
1.9 billion years ago

The earliest **multi-celled** life forms develop.

NOVEMBER 4
720 million years ago

Another long **Ice Age** lasting 50 million years freezes much of the planet.

Rodinia, a giant **supercontinent** forms. It will break up in 250–300 million years.

OCTOBER 4
1.1 billion years ago

NOVEMBER 19
530 million years ago

Early **fish** swim in the oceans. Some are among the first creatures with a backbone.

NOVEMBER 24
465 million years ago

Plants start to grow on land.

The age of the dinosaurs dominating life on land begins. Dinosaurs will only last a further **11 days** in Earth's year of history.

DECEMBER 15
200 million years ago

DECEMBER 19
150 million years ago

The first **birds** develop from species of feathered dinosaurs.

ECEMBER 13
50 million ears ago

The first **dinosaurs** evolve from reptiles.

DECEMBER 21
130 million years ago

Flowering plants appear.

The early continents join to form the supercontinent **Pangea**.

ECEMBER 7
300 million years ago

Our human species, **Homo sapiens**, appears.

DECEMBER 31
300,000 years ago

23:25
20 SECONDS

The first **apes** evolve from monkeys. Some types will later develop into gorillas and the ancestors of **humans**.

DECEMBER 29
25 million years ago

A giant **asteroid** crashes to Earth. It causes climate change and the **extinction** of the dinosaurs.

DECEMBER 26
65 million years ago

DECEMBER 31
2560 BCE

23:59
27 SECONDS

Building work starts on **Egypt's Great Pyramid.**

DECEMBER 31
776 BCE

23:59
40 SECONDS

The first Olympic Games take place in ancient Greece.

DECEMBER 31
117 CE

23:59
46 SECONDS

The Roman Empire peaks in size during the reign of Emperor Trajan.

23:59
54 SECONDS

5...
1347–1351
The Black Death reaches Europe, killing millions of people.

23:59
55 SECONDS

Every single person that is currently alive on the planet was born in the last second of the year.

1...
1969
The first Moon landing.

23:59
59 SECONDS

2...
1789
Start of the French Revolutio

23:5 57 SECON

3...
1603
Shakespeare's play *Hamlet* is printed.

23:59
56 SECONDS

4...
1492
Columbus first sails across the Atlantic to islands in the

Discover more

BOOKS

Animal Record Breakers: Thousands of Amazing Facts and Spectacular Feats
Jane Wisbey (Foreword: Mark Carwardine) Firefly Books. 2016.
Published in conjunction with the Natural History Museum, this book is packed with the longest, heaviest, fastest and loudest creatures on the planet.

Mega Machine Record Breakers
Anne Rooney. Carlton Kids. 2014.
The lowdown on lifters, cranes, diggers and other big machines in this photo-packed book.

Amazing Animals 2018
Guinness World Records Publishing. 2017.
A fun compendium of some of the most astonishing animals on the planet.

Science: A Children's Encyclopedia
Chris Woodford and Steve Parker. Dorling Kindersley. 2014.
From gravity to atoms, from heat to machines, this is a good source for science explanations.

Oceans In 30 Seconds
Jen Green. Ivy Kids. 2015
Dive deep into the world's seas and oceans with this book packed with facts and explanations.

Cars, Trains, Ships and Planes
Clive Gifford. Dorling Kindersley. 2015.
Get all the facts and figures on hundreds of different vehicles in this bumper book.

Operation Ouch!: The HuManual
Ben Elcomb, Dr Chris van Tulleken and Dr Xand van Tulleken. Puffin. 2017
A fun and informative guide to all parts of the human body.

Infopedia 2018
National Geographic Kids. 2017
A rich, fun and detailed encyclopaedia about nature, technology, animals and much more.

The Kingfisher Space Encyclopedia
Dr Mike Goldsmith. Kingfisher. 2017
An excellent 160-page guide to space, the planets and the Universe.

WEBSITES

http://www.bluebulbprojects.com/measureofthings/default.php
Home of the fun The Measure Of Things online app where you can type in a measurement and see it compared to a wide range of other items.

http://www.bbc.co.uk/earth/columns/record-breakers
Stories and facts from the BBC Earth team about different extreme events, places and living things.

https://wmo.asu.edu/content/world-meteorological-organization-global-weather-climate-extremes-archive
Home of the World Meteorological Organisation's archive, this is a key site to visit for global and regional weather records.

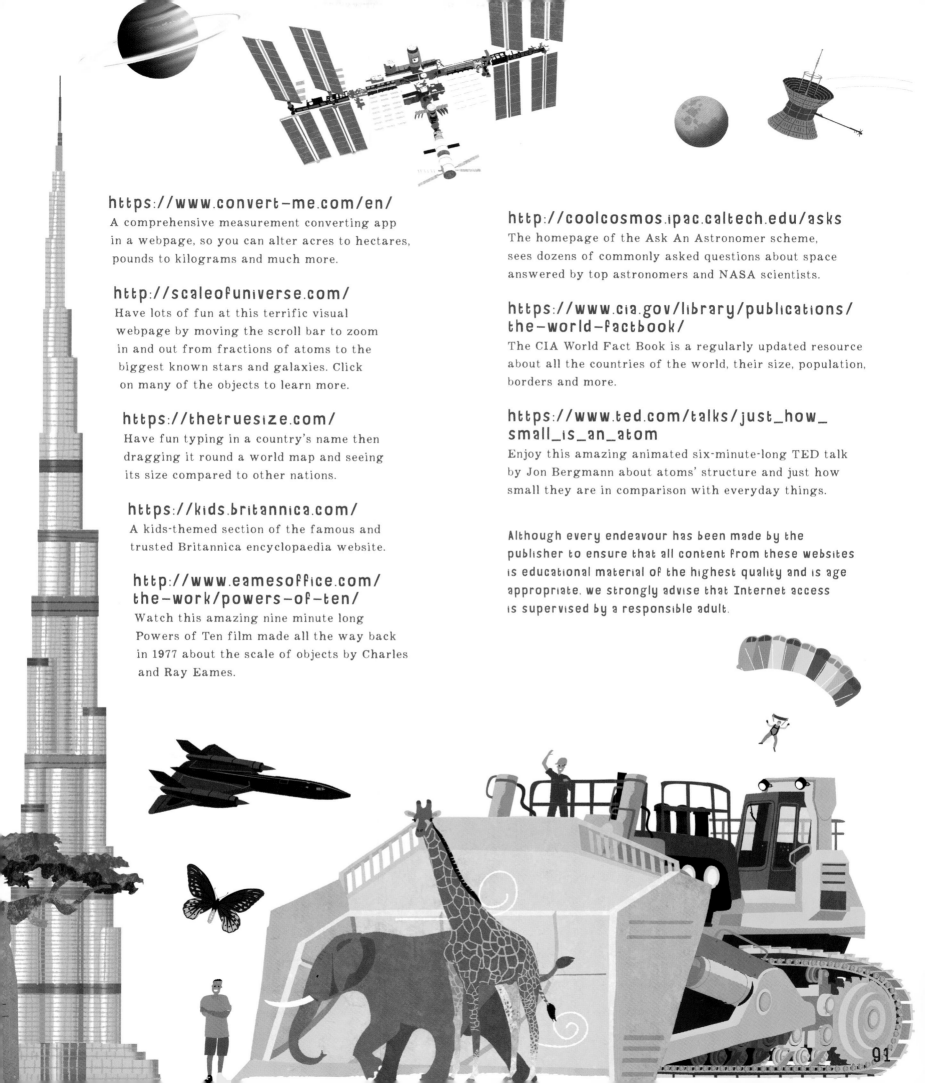

https://www.convert-me.com/en/
A comprehensive measurement converting app
in a webpage, so you can alter acres to hectares,
pounds to kilograms and much more.

http://scaleofuniverse.com/
Have lots of fun at this terrific visual
webpage by moving the scroll bar to zoom
in and out from fractions of atoms to the
biggest known stars and galaxies. Click
on many of the objects to learn more.

https://thetruesize.com/
Have fun typing in a country's name then
dragging it round a world map and seeing
its size compared to other nations.

https://kids.britannica.com/
A kids-themed section of the famous and
trusted Britannica encyclopaedia website.

http://www.eamesoffice.com/
the-work/powers-of-ten/
Watch this amazing nine minute long
Powers of Ten film made all the way back
in 1977 about the scale of objects by Charles
and Ray Eames.

http://coolcosmos.ipac.caltech.edu/asks
The homepage of the Ask An Astronomer scheme,
sees dozens of commonly asked questions about space
answered by top astronomers and NASA scientists.

https://www.cia.gov/library/publications/
the-world-factbook/
The CIA World Fact Book is a regularly updated resource
about all the countries of the world, their size, population,
borders and more.

https://www.ted.com/talks/just_how_
small_is_an_atom
Enjoy this amazing animated six-minute-long TED talk
by Jon Bergmann about atoms' structure and just how
small they are in comparison with everyday things.

Although every endeavour has been made by the
publisher to ensure that all content from these websites
is educational material of the highest quality and is age
appropriate, we strongly advise that Internet access
is supervised by a responsible adult.

Index

How we decided on sizes

Some comparators have measurements that always stay the same – like the height of the Leaning Tower of Pisa in Italy (unless it keeps sinking...). But some comparators have measurements that vary. Even things that we make – such as beach balls or pencils – are not always the same size. So how do you decide how many giraffes it would take to reach the height of the Leaning Tower of Pisa? Usually, you would take the 'average' height of each giraffe.

Averages can be worked out in three different ways:

· Median: this way, you take the range of giraffe heights, from smallest to largest, and use the measurement that is right in the middle.
· Mean: this way, you add up the heights of all giraffes and then divide by how many giraffes there are. This gives each of them an equal measurement.
· Mode: this way, you look at the most usual height for a giraffe and go for that measurement.

It would be too difficult to find out exactly how many giraffes there are in the world and measure them all – the mean average wouldn't work, and the median would be unreliable too. Lots of giraffes have already been measured, so in this case the best method to work out the average would be the mode.

Comparing things is not a precise science – it's rare that a comparison is absolutely exact – usually it's 'around' or 'almost' or 'just over'. But sometimes, when you have two very fixed measurements (such as the length of a pencil and the distance to the moon), you can give an exact figure, and that is very satisfying!

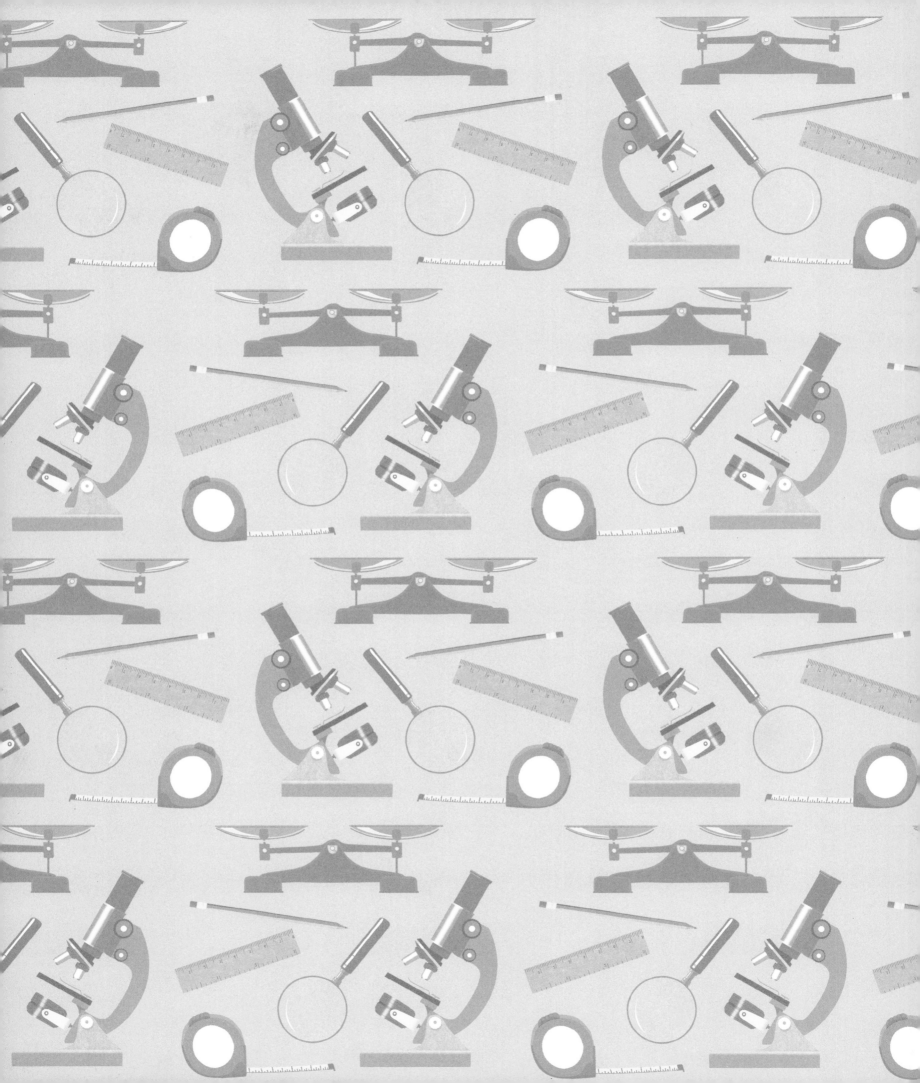